Confidentiality and Record Keeping in Counselling and Psychotherapy

Tim Bond and Barbara Mitchels

SAGE

Los Angeles • London • New Delhi • Singapore • Washington DC

First published 2008

SAGE Publications Ltd
1 Oliver's Yard
55 City Road
London EC1Y 1SP

SAGE Publications Inc.
2455 Teller Road
Thousand Oaks, California 91320

SAGE Publications India Pvt Ltd
B 1/I 1 Mohan Cooperative Industrial Area
Mathura Road
New Delhi 110 044

SAGE Publications Asia-Pacific Pte Ltd
33 Pekin Street #02-01
Far East Square
Singapore 048763

Library of Congress Control Number: 2008920957

British Library Cataloguing in Publication data

A catalogue record for this book is available from
the British Library

ISBN 978-1-4129-1269-3
ISBN 978-1-4129-1270-9   (pbk)

Typeset by C&M Digitals (P) Ltd., Chennai, India
Printed and bound in Great Britain by TJ International Ltd, Padstow, Cornwall
Printed on paper from sustainable resources

Contents

List of Tables

List of Examples

Acknowledgements

We are indebted to all the hundreds of therapists from many different backgrounds and settings who have shared their experience of their dilemmas concerning confidentiality and record keeping and how the law has helped or hindered them. There is no way of naming them individually but we hope that they can recognise some of their concerns in how we have developed this book.

Trying to find the answers to some of the questions that have been posed to us has been challenging. We are particularly grateful to Amanpreet Sandhu who conducted the early legal research in her post as Legal Resources Manager at BACP before leaving for a new post in London and to Roisin Higgins for her helpful comments and addition of the Scottish law in the manuscript.

We would also like to express our especial gratitude to Kirstie Adamson and Cindi Bedor, who willingly shared their experience at a crucial time in the development of this book. We thank them for their contribution of Chapters 8 and 10 respectively, and for enhancing the book with their ideas and examples from practice.

Others have also contributed ideas from their practice that have acted as stepping stones in the development of examples. We are grateful to Roger Casemore for an example of an agreement used with his clients and Heather Dale for creating 'records' of sessions.

Above all we are grateful to the staff of BACP, especially to Denise Chaytor, Kathleen Daymond and Wendy Brewer from the Information Section who drew on their experience of answering members' queries to inform us about the issues that we needed to address. We have also relied heavily on the expertise and encouragement of the Professional Conduct Department, especially Grainne Griffin and John O'Dowd.

Finally we want to express our appreciation to BACP, who have sponsored and supported the writing of this book throughout its creation. The ultimate responsibility for its content rests with us as the authors.

Note on jurisdiction. This book covers the law in England Scotland. The law in other countries is covered only where specifically mentioned.

1 Recording Confidences – Walking the Tightrope

I am a reasonably good therapist with many years' experience. My clients are well satisfied with what I offer ... but I do feel nervous about whether what I do is legally correct concerning confidentiality.

I provide counselling in two places. My employer's policy on confidentiality is so different from what I do in my private practice that I cannot see how they can both be right.

I know what I am doing when I am counselling or coaching...I feel confident about when I need to get extra support. When the law is mentioned I feel exactly the opposite. The law seems so big and I feel so small in comparison that I feel uncertain, anxious and watch myself becoming defensive.

To make things simple I have decided to treat everything my clients tell me as absolutely confidential. It's worked so far but I know that one day it may get me into trouble. I have had a few awkward moments and think that I ought to get clearer about what the law requires.

I don't keep any records – am I wrong?

These are some of the comments made by therapists when we consulted them about how they approach confidentiality and record keeping in their practice. Few issues raise greater anxiety for counsellors and psychotherapists than the appropriate management of their clients' confidences, particularly where a client's trust is at risk. Well managed good practice concerning confidentiality and record keeping can strengthen the therapeutic relationship as trust is deepened and clients feel increasingly secure and respected. This is critically important in counselling and psychotherapy, where clients need to feel able to discuss sensitive thoughts and issues without worrying that they might be communicated to others in ways that could harm them by damaging their reputation or upsetting others. Therefore therapy is usually possible only where there is a high degree of respect for clients' confidences and privacy. On the other hand, badly managed confidentiality and record keeping can have the completely opposite effect, destroying ways of working together and leaving the client feeling betrayed, hurt and misunderstood and the therapist's reputation or integrity undermined. It is not surprising that confidentiality is one of the issues most frequently raised by therapists. This indicates both its importance to everyday practice and the level of difficulty involved in managing it well.

On an issue of such importance to therapists and their clients, it is both reasonable and professionally responsible to turn to the law for guidance. For many therapists, this is where the problems begin. Those who hope for clear and unequivocal guidance leading to certainty will be disappointed in most legal systems based on English and Scottish law or closely related legal systems. Instead of precise rules that can be automatically applied, the law operates as a framework in which professionals, including therapists, are required to exercise a degree of judgement in how they apply the law to the specific circumstances of their work. It is also an area of law where therapists may receive contradictory advice from different sources. Our aim, in writing this book, is to provide information for therapists so that they can base their judgement on a reasonable degree of knowledge about the essential legal framework and understand the complexities and points of tension within the existing law.

Confidentiality and record keeping have been combined in a single book because the two issues are often experienced as increasingly existing in tension with each other. One therapist memorably likened recording her clients' confidence to 'walking a tightrope … wearing a blindfold'. She worked in a service for young people and their parents which had seen a steadily increasing number of requests for copies of clients' records from lawyers for use as evidence in court cases and growing pressures on therapists to co-operate more closely with other professionals. As she reflected on these pressures in her work, she observed,

> I feel that I am walking a tightrope. So long as I stay on the rope I am OK but keeping my balance can be difficult. If I wobble too much towards either side I will fall off. If I lean too far in one direction, by keeping the briefest possible records to protect my client's confidences, I reduce my competence to help my client because my records become too skimpy to help me deliver the therapy. If I lean too far towards on the other side by keeping over-detailed records, I may compromise my client's privacy when I am required to reveal those records. It feels like a balancing act. Sometimes I feel that I am walking the tightrope wearing a blindfold because I cannot always identify what is legally expected of me.

In this book, we hope to be able to remove the 'blindfold' by adequately explaining the relevant law. We will set out the legal frameworks that apply to confidentiality and record keeping in order to help therapists develop and review their practice in ways that are compatible with the law. Because of the current state of the law, we may not be able to eliminate the difficulty of balancing competing legal responsibilities and conflicting legal opinions. We intend that well informed therapists will be able to use the law to support their work and to resist unjustified intrusions into their clients' confidentiality and privacy. Knowing the law is no substitute for being a competent therapist. However, competent therapists who are knowledgeable about the law are best placed to establish some of the essential conditions from which to deliver the highest quality therapy.

Using this book

Throughout the book we have included quotations at the start of chapters from therapists, clients and service managers. Gathered over the last three years' these illustrate the range of views on confidentiality and record keeping. They have influenced the way we have presented the legal information and analysis which is designed to be easily applied by therapists. We have deliberately avoided the traditional style of legal textbooks written for lawyers, but will include references to them where they provide useful sources of further information. We are particularly interested in understanding how the law works in practice. It is seldom more complex than when therapists are working within large organisations with multiple responsibilities to their service users and the community as a whole.

We developed the structure of the book for busy therapists. Some may read the book from cover to cover, but we imagine that most will pick topics of particular relevance to whatever issue is causing concern or is of interest. To meet most needs we have attempted to ensure that each chapter is complete in itself, even if this sometimes means some repetition between chapters or including cross-references to other sources in the book. The best way of navigating around the book will be to use the contents page or index. There are inevitably technical terms in any area of law. We have attempted to keep these to a minimum and have provided a glossary to briefly explain the important ones.

In order to draw on relevant experience, we invited contributions from two therapists with experience and expertise in some of the most problematic aspects of recording confidences. In Chapter 8, Kirstie Adamson draws on her experience as a lawyer and counsellor to provide a case study about writing records and some of the pitfalls. Cindi Bedor uses her experience as manager and team leader to provide a case study in Chapter 10 about how a team of employee counsellors developed their policy and practice for recording their clients' confidences.

Importance of obtaining legal advice

Breaches of confidence and poor record keeping can incur legal liabilities or penalties. There is no substitute for obtaining good up to date legal advice on any issues that are of importance to you or your service. The law is constantly developing and frequently legal opinion depends on the precise circumstances of a particular case. Many professional bodies and insurance services provide access to legal advice or can guide you on where to find the best available sources.

This book should not be used as substitute for obtaining advice from a lawyer. It is intended to help readers understand the broader legal issues concerning confidentiality and record keeping. It may also help managers, practitioners and clients to recognise when there are significant issues at stake that require specific legal advice or to understand the advice that has been given to them.

Defining key terms

There are many technical terms used in the law concerning professional confidentiality and record keeping. We have provided explanations of these terms in a glossary but three terms are so fundamental to understanding this topic that they merit consideration in this introduction. These key terms are 'confidentiality', 'privacy' and 'records'. Each of these terms takes on technical meanings in law that differ from their use in everyday life or their routine practice by counsellors and psychotherapists. In this section, we consider their legal meaning and applications.

Confidentiality

To confide in someone is to put your trust in that person. The origins are Latin with *con-* acting as an intensifier of *fidere* to trust or put one's faith in, and is thus probably best translated as 'to strongly trust someone'. Confidentiality presupposes trust between two people within a community of at least three people. For example, confidentiality occurs when two people decide to restrict the communication of information to between themselves in order to prevent it being communicated to a third person or more people. In a professional relationship, 'confidentiality' means protecting information that could only be disclosed at some cost to another's privacy in order to protect that privacy from being compromised any further. In her extended consideration of *The Law of Professional– Client Confidentiality*, Rosemary Pattenden observed that recent developments in the law have removed the need for a relationship of trust as a prior condition to create legally binding confidentiality. All that is necessary is that the professional was aware, or a reasonable person in her position would have been aware, that the information is private to the subject of that information (Pattenden, 2003: 13).

Privacy

The *Shorter Oxford Dictionary* defines 'privacy' as the 'state or condition of being withdrawn from the society of others or from public attention; freedom from disturbance or intrusion; seclusion …' (Trumble & Stevenson, 2002). The ordinary meaning of the word closely matches its legal use. In contrast to confidentiality which requires at least three people, privacy only requires that one person be able to keep information to him or herself. It can exist in a world without trust and may take on its greatest significance in circumstances of mistrust. It is a more fundamental condition than confidentiality, in that privacy does not require confidentiality but confidentiality requires privacy. For such a core concept in the relationship between people and the relationship between the public and private spheres of life, it is surprisingly hard to be more precise than the dictionary definition in either everyday life or in law. It is a right that has gained significance with the growth of cities and urbanisation, where it is possible to live anonymously and with sufficient independence from others. Discussion of the legal origins of privacy goes back a hundred years in the USA in the case of *Body v US* [1885] (see Pattenden, 2003: 7). 'Breach of confidence' has long been a concept in English law, but notions of privacy became particularly significant when the Human Rights Act 1998 bound the courts to apply the law in compliance with the Human Rights Act 1998 and the European Convention on Human Rights (ECHR), which includes Article 8, the right to privacy. Accordingly, the courts are currently endeavouring to apply the common law provisions of the law of confidence in a way which protects the Article 8 right to privacy – see, for example, the speech of Lord Nicholls in *Campbell v Mirror Group Newspapers* (2004), and the decision in *Douglas v Hello!* (2007).

Records

When therapists refer to 'records' they are typically thinking of any notes they keep about their work with their clients.

There are many possible options for record keeping and their respective advantages and disadvantages are considered in the chapters that follow. Here are just a few examples of the systems that we have seen in practice:

- *Single file system*: All records concerning a single client are kept together in one file, i.e. name, contact details, correspondence, session notes and finances.
- *Two file systems*: The client's name, and details of any financial transactions, are kept together in one file; contact details, correspondence and sessions are kept separately. An alternative approach to keeping two files is to store client names and contact details with correspondence and notes of sessions in one file, and to keep financial information in a different file for accounting and taxation purposes.
- *Multiple file systems*: Client names and contact details in one place; finances kept in another for accounting and taxation purposes; correspondence and notes of sessions kept separately to maximise client privacy. Additional files may be used for other records such as audio recordings, items created by the therapist or client during the session, or notes to be presented in supervision.

The legal meaning of records encompasses all these different approaches to records but stretches further than what is usually thought of as the formal client record. The legal meaning of records may include a diary in which appointments have been made; any surviving jottings on scrap paper made before writing the case notes; the client's drawing or writing made in a therapy session; emails about the work with the client; and notes prepared for discussion in supervision, research or training. A record is any form of document, whether paper-based or electronic, and therefore could include audio or video recordings, recorded telephone messages, computerised charts and photographs. The courts require the best evidence possible, and so the greatest legal weight is given to records made closest in time to the event to which they relate. The extent to which the law will be interested in records beyond those contained in a therapist's file about a specific client will depend on the circumstances.

Should lawyers request a copy of the client records, the file of case notes will usually be adequate for providing evidence to the courts about therapy where the legal issues concern matters between the client and a third party, for example where the client is suing someone following an accident, or where an employer is blamed for an industrial injury. If a client is suing the therapist, the quest for notes may be more wide-ranging and could reasonably include any separately recorded process notes that reveal the therapist's subjective responses as well as any supervision notes. A criminal inquiry might wish to explore all possible documentary sources both for their content as well as for any potential forensic evidence, such as fingerprints and DNA, that might be gathered from those documents or indeed any other sources. Further information about disclosure of records can be found in volume one of our series, *Therapists in Court: Providing Evidence and Supporting Witnesses* (Bond & Sandhu, 2005).

The imprecise and inclusive way that lawyers refer to records means that therapists are well advised to clarify with lawyers what is being referred to and whether records are confined to the client's case file.

Information is the currency of everyday life. In *Commissioner of Police* v. *Ombudsman* (1998) it was defined as 'that which informs, instructs, tells or makes aware'. However, it is the nature of the information that is shared in counselling and psychotherapy that makes the practices of record keeping, confidentiality and privacy so critical and interlocked. The information that clients disclose in therapy is typically both intimate and personal to the client. For this reason we start with the client's perspective in the next chapter.

2 A Right to Confidentiality – the Clients' Perspective

Clients' needs and expectations

I want to be able to take confidentiality for granted. I want to be able to talk freely. I don't want to be distracted by worries about confidentiality.

I don't think that I gave confidentiality a thought when I saw my counsellor. I had so much to talk about and had waited several weeks to get started. I was pouring it all out almost before I sat down.

I am a very private person and don't find talking about personal issues easy. I need to know that there is confidentiality about whatever I say.

What I wanted to talk about is so personal that I really don't want anyone else to know about it unless I tell them. It could affect both my family and my work so I need to be in control.

You know I haven't given confidentiality much thought. My counsellor is clearly careful to be ethical and respectful of me. I trust her to do what she thinks is right for me or to discuss it with me if she is uncertain or sees a problem arising.

When I first saw my counsellor I was so desperate that I was talking to anyone who would listen: friends, neighbours and even strangers in bus queues. I didn't care who knew. I just needed help.

When I was looking for a therapist I wanted the three Cs – someone who is caring, confidential and competent. I couldn't imagine a good experience of therapy without all three being present. I needed all three personal qualities to be present, as a serious deficiency in any one of these would undermine the others and give me a false sense of security.

These comments present a variety of views about the significance of confidentiality to clients. They reveal that there are no standard needs in relation to confidentiality. 'A very private person' may want absolute confidentiality to feel safe. A very troubled person may be willing to disregard confidentiality in the urgency of seeking help which has become an overwhelming priority. For all, confidentiality is not the primary purpose of therapy but a necessary condition that makes therapy possible. Without an expectation of confidentiality, most of these clients would either have felt constrained in what they could say to their therapist or that it would be too risky to engage in therapy until the need for therapy overwhelms sensible self-protection.

For the client there is potentially a lot at stake. Personal information in the wrong hands can be very damaging to personal relationships, employment and public reputation in the wider community. Clients are taking a risk in talking to a therapist and it is only the expectation of confidentiality that makes this risk acceptable. Many clients may want to discuss sensitive personal information about themselves and they may also give information about other people involved in the events they want to discuss. Furthermore, the process of therapy may expose other information that had not previously been put into words, typically troubling feelings and the impact of difficult experiences. In order to be able to deepen their sense of themselves and to discover the personal resourcefulness to enhance their lives, clients need to be able to trust the therapist to respect and protect their confidences.

It is understandable that clients who are concerned about confidentiality desire simplicity, straightforwardness and predictability backed by high levels of certainty over such a sensitive issue. The diversity of backgrounds of clients also favours a basis for confidentiality that is simple enough to be easily communicated and readily understood by people with different abilities and experiencing various levels of distress so that clients are not distracted from their primary purpose in coming to therapy: that is, to receive help. Words need to mean what they seem to mean and not be subject to lots of exceptions and interpretations or to be contradicted by actual practice. Clients need to know that what is offered at the outset will reliably predict what will follow. With enough certainty about what is being offered, confidentiality takes its proper place by providing clients with sufficient safety and protection from the risk of having difficulties and sensitivities exposed to others. A straightforward and robust approach to confidentiality leaves the client much better placed to talk frankly, with only their own personal constraints and internal censors to limit what can be said. Some clients may hope for absolute confidentiality and total control over what is disclosed in therapy.

A fantasy of what would be legally required to provide total protection of clients' confidences

The purpose of this brief excursion into legal fantasy is to explore what the law might look like if it were to meet a client's needs for simplicity, straightforwardness and certainty about almost total protection of their confidences. We offer this example of an imaginary Therapeutic Secrets Act written entirely with the purpose of protecting clients' confidences in order to highlight the types of issue that have led to the current complexity of the law that is challenging for both clients and therapists alike. A law that sought only to protect clients' confidences might contain the following provisions:

- An obligation of strict confidentiality would be placed on all recipients of personally sensitive information disclosed during therapy.
- Disclosure of therapeutic confidences would only be permitted with the client's explicit consent in circumstances that ensure that the consent has been conscientiously sought and given.

- Wrongful disclosure of therapeutic confidences would be a serious punishable offence regardless of the intentions of the person making the disclosure, and the client would be entitled to compensation for any harm caused.
- Legal privilege would be granted for therapeutic confidences in order to protect them from disclosure to any court or law officers.

This imaginary legal framework would provide a high degree of certainty and security over the protection of confidences that is superficially attractive. It would provide excellent legal protection of clients' confidences but could compromise the provision of good therapy intended to serve the client's well-being in other ways:

- How can clients' confidences be protected without preventing therapists from receiving training and professional support intended to promote the quality of service on offer to their clients?
- What are the limits of managing confidentiality solely on the basis of client consent? How should therapists respond to people who are incapable of expressing what they want due to their immaturity, intoxication, disability, illness or extreme distress? How should therapists work with people whose autonomy is disrupted by their vulnerability created by any of these circumstances?
- When is it appropriate for therapists to breach confidentiality against the wishes of the clients in order to prevent clients inflicting serious harm to themselves such as self-mutilation or suicide?
- At what point ought a therapist to intervene to protect a client who is unwilling or unable to protect themselves from abuse by others, such as child or elder abuse?
- When is it appropriate to override clients' confidentiality in order to investigate suspected misconduct or the exploitation of clients by therapists?

Such a single-minded protection of client confidentiality could require an extraordinary degree of self-sacrifice by therapists where their professional and personal well-being could be sacrificed to preserving client confidentiality. For example:

- When is it appropriate for therapists to breach a client's confidences in order to protect themselves from being harassed or endangered by a client? Such instances are fortunately rare but have been seriously harmful to the therapists concerned, who have been stalked, assaulted and on very rare occasions murdered. Services to other clients may also have been disrupted or diminished in quality.

Similarly, the protection of client confidentiality may be gained at the cost of preventing harm to others:

- When is it appropriate to breach confidentiality in order to prevent a client inflicting serious harm on another person? At what point is the client's right to confidentiality overridden by the rights of others?

There is also the question of the balance between the good that can be achieved by providing therapy on a confidential basis and the overall well-being of society as a whole:

- Where does the balance lie between avoiding deterring people from seeking therapy because of fear of breaches of confidentiality, and the benefits to society in enabling the investigation and detection of serious crime even when this requires therapists to breach confidences?
- At what point do the principles of justice and fairness between citizens require that any court cases are decided on the basis of all the relevant information being made available to the court, even if this means intruding on what would otherwise be confidential to the persons concerned? In some situations such cases may be observed by members of the public or reported by the press, which extends the intrusion on what has originally been disclosed in confidence. Should information disclosed in therapeutic confidence be given legal privilege to protect it from being required to be disclosed in court cases?

This list of issues indicates the potential for complexity when confidentiality is considered in the wider context of competing interests in society. It is not surprising therefore that our fantasy of a Therapeutic Secrets Act is just that: a fantasy. It is unlikely ever to become a legal reality. In so far as law is a form of public morality, there are competing moral interests that impact in different ways on the provision of confidentiality. The protection of a client's confidences is a significant moral issue but it is not the only one. How competing interests are resolved concerning confidentiality varies between different legal systems and changes over time within any legal system in response to pressing social issues, changes in public morality and the persuasive powers of those affected.

This means that any client's desires for total simplicity, straightforwardness and certainty with regard to confidentiality are unlikely to be met. There will always be a degree of uncertainty about how confidentiality within therapy will be managed in response to competing moral and legal principles. Nonetheless it is reasonable for clients to desire basic information about how their confidences will be protected, and in most cases the management of confidentiality proves to be more straightforward in practice than the potential complexity of law developed to consider all eventualities would suggest. In the next section, we outline in general terms the general legal principles that are applicable in England and Scotland and increasingly across Europe.

What level of protection of confidences can clients expect in reality?

The psychological therapies have a longstanding concern with protecting client confidences but therapists' legal obligations with regard to confidentiality are essentially the same as those of any professional who acquires sensitive personal information about others during the course of their work. In this respect therapists are no different from medics, dentists, nurses, accountants, ministers of religion, social workers or teachers with regard to confidentiality. The current law provides a considerable degree of protection for confidences disclosed in therapy.

Firstly, there is a strong legal entitlement to confidentiality that protects personal information acquired during therapy and attendance at therapy from unauthorised disclosure. The entitlement to confidentiality exists even if the therapist is silent on this point. It is a right that can be legally enforced and protected by legal orders, payment of damages, and by professional and organisational disciplinary procedures. However, confidentiality is never protected as an absolute right in English and Scottish law. The right to confidentiality is enforced as a matter of benefit to society. Legally this is expressed as being in the 'public interest' and therefore may be overridden where the public interest would justify this.

Secondly, there is a strong professional and legal assumption that clients ought to be informed in general terms about any limitations to confidentiality and that disclosures of confidentiality ought to be managed on the basis of the client's informed consent. Typical limitations to confidentiality include:

- Prevention of serious physical harm to clients or others.
- Any legal requirements to breach confidentiality, including court orders and statutory obligations.
- Any disclosures required to enhance the quality of service offered by the therapist, e.g. obtaining professional supervision and support or sharing information with colleagues within a team setting. For further discussion see Chapter 9.

Thirdly, a client's rights of control over personal information held about them have been strengthened by data protection legislation that requires a client's explicit consent to the compilation of most types of records of sensitive information and gives the client the right to see any records that have been made and to ensure that they are kept safely (see Chapter 5). The right to privacy granted by the Human Rights Act 1998 may also strengthen a client's claim to confidentiality.

Fourthly, clients are generally entitled to be informed of any breaches of confidentiality, regardless of whether these were accidental or deliberate following careful consideration, unless there are grounds of public interest or legal obligations that prevent the client being informed. Where clients are entitled to information about a disclosure of confidential information, they should be told what was disclosed, to whom and when, as soon as is reasonably possible after the event.

Finally, although it is not strictly a legal requirement, most therapists will want to know about any specific concerns about confidentiality that might inhibit a client's participation in therapy in order to examine whether these can resolved by mutual agreement.

Exactly how therapists meet these legal requirements in practice will vary. Some will address confidentiality through discussion with the client. Agreements reached by oral discussion are legally valid but are vulnerable to misunderstanding and are weak as evidence in the event of any dispute. Some therapists provide information sheets or a letter after an initial appointment that states how confidentiality will be managed. Others provide statements of the general responsibilities held respectively by a client and therapist which will include issues concerning confidentiality. Some place greater emphasis on outlining most eventualities at the beginning of the therapeutic relationship whereas others raise issues as they become relevant to the way therapy is unfolding.

In this chapter we have addressed some typical concerns over confidentiality from the clients' perspective. We have sought to establish why absolute confidentiality is not legally enforceable and why some aspects of confidentiality may seem unduly complex within the existing legal framework. We have concluded with a statement of what clients might reasonably expect from legally conscientious therapists. In the next chapters we examine the legal basis of managing confidences in greater depth, with particular attention to the legal issues and principles that ought to underpin the therapist's practice.

3 Confidentiality as a Legal Responsibility – Obligations of the Therapist

These are some of the comments about confidentiality that we have heard from therapists:

I want to be a psychotherapist and be listening for what will heal. Instead I find the current state of the law is so complex and unpredictable in its consequences that at least part of my mind is listening for potential difficulties over confidentiality. It gets in the way.

When we first started counselling people affected by HIV and AIDS, the moral panic was at its height. Our clients were frightened and felt very vulnerable to public prejudice, often with good cause. We became so concerned with issues of confidentiality that it was almost becoming the primary purpose of our service until we pulled ourselves up short and asked what are we here for? We are not offering consultation in confidentiality but psychological support and therapy.

I don't experience many problems with confidentiality. I am clear with my clients about what I can offer and the limitations of what I can keep confidential. If they want a service that's the way I do it. Occasionally some clients want more confidentiality than I offer and they have to choose whether to work with me on my terms or look elsewhere.

Keep it simple. I offer absolute confidentiality and would be prepared to go to prison to protect this.

The most difficult issue I experience is clients asking me to disclose information on their behalf when I don't think it is in their interests to do so or feel that it will damage our therapeutic relationship.

I just don't feel secure in my practice on this topic. I have tried to alert clients to all the potential restrictions on confidentiality before we start but often it is irrelevant and looks more like a legal seminar, which frustrates them and me. If I keep it simple, I can find myself being given information by inadequately informed clients who tell me things without realising that they have opened up ethical and legal dilemmas for both of us. With this client group, they can be exposing themselves to potentially serious consequences outside of therapy.

I feel the reputation of our service depends on being confidential, especially in a situation like this where everyone knows everyone else. If we don't get that right, there won't be any clients.

Confidentiality is about managing information in ways that keep it secure and control its disclosure. It is concerned with protecting information that is identifiable with a specific person, typically because the person is named, but the law will also protect the confidences of people whose identity can be deduced from the available information, perhaps because the listener knows some of the circumstances of the person being referred to. Thoroughly anonymised information in which the identity of specific people cannot be discerned is not protected by the law of confidentiality.

Confidentiality is a wide-ranging duty that applies to anyone in their personal or professional life. So therapists are not unique in their legal obligations, but the nature of the work makes this a particularly sensitive issue. In this chapter we concentrate on those aspects of the law that are most likely to be encountered in counselling, psychotherapy and psychology. This is one of the most rapidly developing areas of law and there have been very significant developments over the last ten years both in case law, that is the law created by the courts, and also by legislation, particularly the Human Rights Act 1998 and the Data Protection Act 1998, both of which will be referred to throughout the rest of this book. One of the consequences of these developments, particularly the strengthening of the relationship between confidentiality and privacy, has been to simplify and widen the circumstances in which a legal obligation of confidentiality will arise. In one of the most comprehensive studies of the law of professional–client confidentiality, Rosemary Pattenden provides a useful summary of the impact of these developments.

> A professional (like anyone else) who somehow acquires confidential personal information may be saddled with an obligation of confidentiality toward X, the subject of the information, whether there was a direct, indirect or no contact with X. All that is necessary is that the professional was aware, or a reasonable person in her position would have been aware, that the information is private to X. (Pattenden, 2003: 13)

As a result of these developments, therapists have wider obligations than simply protecting private information disclosed directly by their clients. Information given by someone about a potential client in the process of making a referral is also covered by a duty of confidentiality even though this is an indirect communication about the person concerned. The knowledge that someone might require or is seeking therapy is a private matter. Similarly, information sent in error about a client to the wrong therapist also creates a duty of confidentiality, even though there has been no contact between the therapist and client nor is any future contact intended. A legally wise response to this situation would be to notify the sender of the error, assuring them that the information is being treated as confidential, and to ask their guidance on whether they would like it securely returned or destroyed.

The critical question in determining whether a duty of confidentiality has been created depends on the answer to whether there is a reasonable expectation of privacy. Lord Woolf examined how the right to privacy is now protected by the law of confidentiality following the Human Rights Act 1998 and brought these two elements together in a statement about how a duty of confidentiality arises.

A duty of confidence will arise whenever the party subject to the duty is in a situation where he either knows or ought to know that the other person can reasonably expect his privacy to be protected. (See *A* v. *B plc and C ('Flitcroft')* [2002]).

We will take this statement as the basis for examining the extent of therapists' obligations in terms of confidentiality. It becomes apparent that any disclosure of personal information to a therapist satisfies this test on several grounds, including the following:

1 *The circumstances in which the information was disclosed*: Counselling and psychotherapy are strongly associated with a robust ethic of client confidentiality. The ethical requirements and guidance offered by the leading professional bodies also stress confidentiality (BACP, 2007: 6 para. 16; BPS, 2006: 1.2; IACP, 2005: 1.5). The longstanding attentiveness to issues of confidentiality has created a strong public expectation of confidentiality.

2 *The nature of the information itself*: Knowing that someone is receiving counselling or psychotherapy is potentially sufficiently sensitive to be protected by privacy because of its association with someone requiring or seeking help who might otherwise wish to be considered as fully functioning. The content of the therapy may also focus on what are properly regarded as private issues concerning personal relationships, and psychological and physical well-being. For nearly thirty years, the law has taken the view that 'certain kinds of information are categorised as private and ought not to be disclosed' (Law Commission, 1981: para 2.3). In a leading case on confidentiality, *Attorney General* v. *Guardian Newspapers (No 2)* [1988] took the view that some information is 'obviously confidential'. The extra level of statutory protection offered to personal records relating to 'counselling or assistance for the purpose of personal welfare' during police searches (Police and Criminal Evidence Act 1984, section 12) provides a strong indication of how the English law has recognised the confidential nature of therapy for over twenty years.

3 *Personal information disclosed in a relationship of trust*: The existence of a relationship of trust may no longer be required to establish a claim to confidentiality or privacy because a duty of confidentiality can also arise outside a relationship of trust. However, where disclosures of personal information take place in a relationship of trust, the legal presumption of confidentiality is extremely strong. In a New Zealand case, which carries persuasive weight in British courts, Judge Anderson stated:

It should be so obvious as to go without saying that when a person seeking psychological support who consults, even gratuitously as here, a professional psychologist acting in such capacity for psychological advice then the usual confidentiality of a psychologist/ patient relationship must apply. (*JD* v. *Ross* [1998])

For all these reasons, counsellors and psychotherapists owe their clients a legal duty of confidentiality. Any personally identifiable information is to be protected. It does not appear to matter whether the disclosure of information is favourable or unfavourable to the person concerned. Any unauthorised disclosure may be damaging to a client. Disclosures of unfavourable information may damage someone's reputation, with all the consequences that might follow in their personal, work and social opportunities. Even information that is not considered harmful may become damaging to the person concerned due to the reactions of others, by exciting jealousy, rivalry or other problematic reactions. The act of unauthorised disclosure alone may unsettle the relationship between therapist and client as well as the client's peace. The Supreme Court of India observed that disclosure of confidences 'has the tendency to disturb a person's tranquillity. It may generate more complexes in him and he may, thereafter, have a disturbed life all through' (*Mr X v. Hospital Z* [1998]).

This general duty of confidentiality established by the decisions of the courts is further reinforced by the Data Protection Act 1998 and the Human Rights Act 1998 where these apply. These Acts will be considered separately in Chapter 6.

Exceptions to the duty of confidentiality

Although the law imposes a general duty of confidentiality on therapists with regard to personal information about their clients, especially information considered private, there are a number of exceptions to this duty. These are as follows.

Consent

If a client consents to disclosure, the duty of non-disclosure ceases to exist. Seeking a client's explicit consent is legally and ethically the most satisfactory way of resolving dilemmas over confidentiality. The consent may be total or, more likely, quite specific in what may be communicated and to whom. Anything that is not included in the explicit terms of the consent remains protected by an obligation of confidentiality.

Therapists are increasingly working in teams, agencies, or in co-operation with other agencies or organisations. This raises the question of whether clients need to give explicit consent to communications within the team on a confidential basis: see Chapter 9 for a further discussion of sharing information between professionals. Ethically, the optimum practice is generally considered to be seeking the client's explicit consent for these communications and clarifying where the boundary of the obligation of confidentiality lies – typically within an identified group of workers or within the agency. This is widely thought to be most respectful of clients and is a way of establishing the conditions in which to encourage open and candid communications by the client. It also provides an opportunity to establish the client's attitude to confidentiality and whether there are any issues that might otherwise be unknown to the therapist that ought to be taken into consideration. For example, a client may wish to restrict what may be communicated to a member of the team who is the client's relative, neighbour or social acquaintance. This attentiveness to consent is consistent with the personal dimension of the therapist–client relationship in which the therapist is not easily interchangeable with colleagues from one session to another in the way that is possible with physical care such as giving injections or changing dressings. Where roles are interchangeable, there is a stronger case for establishing an expectation that there will be communication within the team in order to improve the quality of care offered and to provide a seamless service; but, even in these circumstances, clients can legally limit what is communicated about them by insisting on their right to confidentiality and privacy.

Where therapists work in multidisciplinary settings, such as a GP's surgery, a social care agency or educational institution, they may find themselves working in a context where the client's implicit consent is considered adequate for disclosure on a confidential basis between colleagues within that setting. Provided the person concerned is aware of this practice of disclosure and has been given the opportunity to object to it, implicit consent is legally sufficient to legitimise the communication of confidential information. Recent developments in information sharing as matter of public policy are considered in Chapter 9.

Balance of public interest

Arguably, the most important exception to the duty of confidentiality arises where there is a public interest in the disclosure of the information, which outweighs the public interest in preserving the client's confidentiality. In common law, the obligation of confidentiality arises because there is a public interest in ensuring that people's confidential information is respected, but this is not an absolute right that persists in all circumstances. There are times when confidentiality has to give way to broader public interest. One key case of relevance to therapy illustrates how the courts view the professional's role in such decisions and how it undertakes the difficult task of balancing the competing interests.

The case of *W* v. *Edgell and others* [1990] concerned someone who suffered from paranoid schizophrenia. In 1974, W had shot and killed five people and injured two others. In 1986, he applied to a mental heath review tribunal to be released from a secure mental health hospital in which he had been detained. The Secretary of State blocked W's release. W's solicitors commissioned an independent assessment and report from Dr Edgell, a consultant psychiatrist. Dr Edgell reported that W had a long-term and ongoing interest in home-made bombs and that he considered that W remained a danger to the public. W's solicitors withdrew his application for release. Even though Dr Edgell was bound by contractual terms of confidentiality when commissioned to undertake this work, he was sufficiently concerned about the potential dangers posed by W to have discussed the case and his concerns with the medical director of the hospital. As a result of these discussions, which were a breach of confidence owed to W and his solicitor, it was agreed that both the hospital and the Secretary of State should receive a copy of the report, further extending the breaches of confidence. When W learned that the report had been passed to the hospital and the tribunal, through the Secretary of State, he started legal actions against Dr Edgell and all the recipients of the report seeking:

- a court order to restrain them from using or disclosing the report,
- the return of all copies of the report, and
- damages for breach of the duty of confidence.

W's case failed in the High Court and his appeal was dismissed by the Court of Appeal.

In his judgment, Lord Justice Bingham reviewed decisions in previous cases and stated, 'The decided cases very clearly establish (1) that the law recognises an important public interest in maintaining professional duties of confidence, but (2) that the law treats such duties not as absolute but as liable to be overridden where there is held to be a stronger public interest in disclosure.' All the judgments viewed the potential seriousness of the dangers as justifying Dr Edgell's breach of confidentiality and his concern that those responsible for providing treatment and managing the care and custody of W should be aware of significant information gathered during his assessment. In many ways the past history and severity of the dangers posed by W made this a relatively easy balancing act. Despite the introduction of the Human Rights Act, a case based on similar circumstances today would be likely to reach the same conclusions in favour of disclosure.

Therapists are often faced with less clear-cut circumstances. Dilemmas over confidentiality concerning harm to other people can arise with clients who have no previous history of harming anyone but are proposing to harm someone in retaliation for some real harm caused to them, or in response to a psychological fantasy. The fact that the therapist is having difficulty containing his or her own anxiety is not a sufficient reason to breach a client's confidentiality. This might justify additional professional support provided on a confidential basis, but may not justify a breach of confidentiality likely to have significant consequences for the client. In making decisions on confidentiality, it may be useful to distinguish between situations when circumstances are of such seriousness that they justify a breach of confidence and situations where the balance of public interest appears to justify disclosure, and to understand the process of how such a decision ought to be undertaken.

There are many different versions of what circumstances ought to be taken into account, both in case law and professional guidance, especially for health workers. What follows is a carefully considered collation of that guidance bearing in mind the high levels of significance attached to the privacy and confidentiality concerning personal information in counselling, psychotherapy and psychology. The circumstances that could justify a breach of confidentiality require that there should be a real risk of serious harm, the threat appears imminent and the disclosure is likely to be effective in limiting or preventing the harm occurring. Each of these criteria is considered in turn.

Real risk   A client who is actively planning something with a precise schedule, or who has advanced further in this by making physical preparations to cause harm, is moving beyond fantasy and into an action stage and, to this extent, could now be posing a real risk. Similarly a client in the grip of uncontrollable rage or psychosis, or who has suppressed their inhibitions by intoxication, could be considered to pose a real risk depending on the other circumstances in the case. A client who has reported experiencing similar intentions to harm others, but has not done so, would represent a lower risk. Whether or not they constitute real risk would depend on how this situation differs from earlier ones. For example, is it more severe or part of a pattern of escalating behaviour?

Serious harm A threat to life, inflicting serious physical harm, rape and child abuse would all be examples of serious harm. The risk of a car accident or the spread of serious disease could amount to serious harm. The prevention of psychological distress or harm without any associated serious physical injury, criminal activity or child protection issue, may not justify a breach of confidentiality in English law, especially for adults and young people of adequate understanding and intelligence capable of giving valid consent. The prevention of psychological harm without other associated harms is best resolved by consent.

Imminent The risk or threat of harm must be sufficiently imminent that those bound by confidentiality are unlikely to be able to take effective preventative action, for example in the course of therapy, and there is little possibility of the risk or threat subsiding with the passage of time because time is running out.

Effective There has to be a reasonable probability that the breach of confidence will minimise or prevent the risk or threat of harm.

The nature of the circumstances in which the risk is discovered will determine the extent to which a therapist can make a carefully considered judgement. For example, courts will accept that someone acting in an urgent situation, under the pressure of an immediately imminent risk, may have less opportunity to investigate any of these criteria than someone who has longer to consult colleagues or others with relevant expertise on an anonymous or confidential basis.

If the therapist considers that the balance of public interest favours disclosure, the next step is to consider how to undertake this in ways that are consistent with the public interest in preserving confidentiality by avoiding unnecessary damage to the client's privacy by:

- Selecting the information to be disclosed: disclosure of information should be limited to that necessary in order to avert the risk.
- Selecting the recipient(s) of the information: disclosure should only be made to a person or agency that is capable of minimising or preventing the harm.

Seeking the client's consent A client's consent provides the best protection both of a client's rights and those of the therapist, unless seeking such consent enhances the risk of harm, will inhibit effective investigation of a serious crime, or the circumstances prevent this. There needs to be a sound reason for not informing a client in advance of an intention to breach confidentiality. If the client refuses consent, their reasons ought to be considered and, if possible, taken into account. General Medical Council guidance to doctors directs, 'If you remain of the view that disclosure is necessary to protect a third party from death or serious harm, you should disclose information promptly to an appropriate person or authority' (GMC, 2004, paragraph 27).

Communicate the information on a confidential basis   Written communications should be marked 'Confidential' or 'In confidence'. Oral communications should be preceded by a clear statement that what is being disclosed is confidential. If the therapist is unfamiliar with the practice of the person or agency receiving the information, it is reasonable to ask how the information will be protected or treated in advance of disclosing it.

Make a record of the decision-making process as soon as practically possible. This is now a standard requirement in most statutory services and serves to mark the seriousness with which someone's privacy and confidentiality is regarded, as well as providing the essential basis for any review by the courts or other agencies of the decision-making process. The probability of a client complaining or initiating litigation following a breach of confidentiality makes this respectful and prudent practice for all therapists.

Notify the client of the communication of confidential information, specifically, what has been communicated to whom, unless there are good reasons for not doing so (for example those that make it inadvisable to seek consent). Where the disclosure concerns serious crime, the law may forbid notifying the person concerned and to do so may be an offence known as 'tipping off' (see p.27 below).

The courts are interested in whether the therapist has taken reasonable care in weighing up where the public interest lies and will take account of the circumstances in which the decision had to be made. They do not expect that all therapists will necessarily agree with the decision. Courts are concerned that the specific decision and actions by the people concerned have been taken with a reasonable level of conscientiousness and respect for the obligation of confidentiality. In situations where there is real risk of physical harm to another, courts should not be over-zealous in proving the therapist wrong (Brazier, 2003: 68).

There is a noticeable difference between the legal reasoning in British and American cases that is reflected in guidance offered by professional bodies. This may be a source of some confusion, as many American textbooks on therapy are read by British therapists. One of the recurrent sources of confusion concerns whether therapists have a duty to warn a third party of dangers posed by one of their clients. In the USA, a client, Poddar, was being seen in a university health centre by a clinical psychologist. Poddar told his therapist that he intended to murder Ms Tarasoff when she returned from a trip to Brazil because he felt rejected by her. The therapist knew of his previous history of violence, that he had also armed himself with a gun, and took his threat seriously. The psychologist consulted with colleagues, unsuccessfully attempted to have Poddar institutionalised, and notified the university police, who briefly detained him but released him because he appeared rational. No one warned the intended victim of the danger she was in. Poddar brutally murdered Ms Tarasoff. Her parents initiated the case of *Tarasoff* v. *The Regents of the University of California* [1974], which is now widely cited in therapeutic literature as establishing a duty to warn third parties. This is an outdated interpretation of this case. The judgment was reconsidered in *Tarasoff II* [1976] which changed the duty from one of having to warn the potential victim to one of taking reasonable steps to protect the person at risk of harm. This revised duty allows the circumstances to be taken into account and could be met in a variety of ways, including warning the person at risk, informing others who are likely to warn the victim, or notifying the police of a potential danger. This duty to act to protect someone from risk of physical harm by a client is stronger in American law than on this side of the Atlantic. The consensus amongst legal commentators is that *Tarasoff* would not be followed in English courts (Jackson, 2006: 342; Pattenden, 2003: 695; Pattinson, 2006: 197).

There is no positive duty in English and Scottish law to warn third parties or to take reasonable steps to protect a potential victim in similar circumstances to Tarasoff, However, British courts would probably regard any beach of confidentiality as justified on the balance of public interest if a therapist did warn a potential victim in similar circumstances or sought the assistance of the appropriate authorities to prevent the harm. In this respect, British therapists retain more opportunities to exercise their professional judgement than their American colleagues.

The prevention and detection of serious crime

This justification for breaches of confidentiality reaches more widely than harm to others, which was considered in the previous section. Although the definition of serious crime is not entirely clear in law the Department of Health has offered the following guidance:

> Murder, manslaughter, rape, treason, kidnapping, child abuse or other cases where individuals have suffered serious harm may all warrant breaching confidentiality. Serious harm to the security of the state or to public order and crimes that involve substantial financial gain and loss will generally fall within this category. In contrast, theft, fraud or damage to property where loss or damage is less substantial would generally not warrant breach of confidence. (DH, 2003a: 35)

The Human Rights Act 1998

The Human Rights Act applies across the United Kingdom, to all 'public authorities', a term which is not defined but includes the courts and tribunals, and therefore has a pervasive influence in all areas of society. There are similar measures in place across most of the European Union and where human rights are protected by the European Court of Human Rights (ECtHR) in terms of the European Convention on Human Rights (ECHR). Article 8 of the ECHR (as set out in Schedule 1 to the Human Rights Act) establishes the 'right to respect for private and family life'. This is not an absolute right. Articles 8.1 and 8.2 ought to be read alongside each other as the second qualifies the rights asserted in the first.

> Article 8.1   Everyone has the right to respect for his private and family life, his home, and his correspondence.

Article 8.2   There shall be no interference by a public authority with the exercise of this right except such as is in accordance with the law and is necessary in a democratic society in the interests of national security, public safety or the economic well-being of the country, for the prevention of disorder or crime, for the protection of health or morals, or for the protection of the rights and freedoms of others.

Although we are not aware of any cases specifically involving privacy in counselling or psychotherapeutic consultations and their records, we would suggest that they are covered both by the wording of Article 8 and by analogy with medical cases. It has not proved especially difficult for individuals to establish that any disclosure of their medical records constitutes a prima facie violation of Article 8 (Jackson, 2006: 323).

The courts have approached cases from the viewpoint of weighing competing interests and deciding where the balance ought to lie. In *Z* v. *Finland* [1998] the ECtHR balanced a wife's right to privacy concerning her medical records against the police need to access those records as part of an investigation into sexual offences by her husband. Specifically they wanted to discover when he became aware of his positive HIV status. The court decided that the personal and community interest protecting the confidentiality of medical records may be outweighed by the interest in the investigation and prosecution of crime. However, it was not considered proportionate to reveal her identity to the public in a Court of Appeal judgment. Similarly in *MS* v. *Sweden* [1999], the court considered that the prevention of benefit fraud outweighed the protection of the privacy of medical records.

As many therapists work in agencies with accountability to management, a case concerning the investigation of a GP may be of interest. The case of *A Health Authority* v. *X* [2001] concerned the investigation by a health authority into a doctor for suspected over-prescribing, incomplete medical records, inappropriate delegation of his responsibilities and failing to obtain adequate medical consent before performing medical procedures. Some patients withheld their consent to disclosure of their medical records. Again the court decided in favour of disclosure, as Lord Justice Thorpe observed, 'as it invariably does, save in exceptional cases'. The proper administration of criminal justice and the proper administration of professional disciplinary hearings justified the release of the records, with conditions of confidentiality imposed on those who received them.

All the Articles in the ECHR have to be held in balance with each other. For example, in a case concerning the treatment of a celebrity, her rights to privacy under Article 8 had to be balanced with the right to freedom of expression under Article 10 which is frequently used by the press to support their right to publish. In *Campbell* v. *MGN Ltd* [2004] the court was asked to consider the rights of a celebrity, the well known fashion model Naomi Campbell. A newspaper had published a story about her drug addiction, her receipt of treatment and her attendance at Narcotics Anonymous. The story was illustrated with photographs of her attending a Narcotics Anonymous meeting. At the final appeal, Naomi Campbell accepted that the press was entitled to contradict her previous claims that she was not a drug addict and that the disclosure of her addiction was in the public interest. However, she disputed the right of the press to publish photographs and information about her attendance at Narcotics Anonymous. The House of Lords agreed with her in a majority verdict of 3: 2.

Naomi Campbell's case was brought for breach of confidence and compensation under the Data Protection Act and illustrates how this legislation may also be used to protect confidentiality. We will consider this legislation in greater detail in Chapter 6.

Legal obligations to breach confidentiality

Court orders

The law offers protection to someone who is legally required to disclose confidences, for example in response to a court order (see Bond & Sandhu, 2005, for further details of requests for confidential information by solicitors, which cannot compel disclosure, and court orders, which can).

Terrorist activities

There is a general duty to report information which assists in the prevention of terrorist activities. The Terrorism Act 2000, s. 38B, makes it a criminal offence for a person to fail to disclose, without reasonable excuse, any information which he either knows or believes might help prevent another person carrying out an act of terrorism or might help in bringing a terrorist to justice in the UK. It is, in our view, unlikely that professional confidentiality would ever be regarded in these circumstances as a reasonable excuse by a court.

Section 39 of the Terrorism Act 2000 creates the separate offence popularly known as 'tipping off'. This offence is committed 'where a person knows or has reasonable cause to suspect that a constable is conducting or proposes to conduct a terrorist investigation' and he

(a) discloses to another anything which is likely to prejudice the investigation, or
(b) interferes with material which is likely to be relevant to the investigation.

The maximum penalty for tipping off is five years' imprisonment, a fine, or both. In addition to (and separate from) the obligations described above under s. 38B of the Terrorism Act 2000, there is a different duty under s. 19 of that Act for all citizens to report any information about specified activities related to money and property used to assist terrorist activities which they have gained through the course of a trade, profession, business or employment.

The duty to report financial and property information learned at home was therefore not included in the Terrorism Act 2000. However, a duty does remain to report information about fundraising (s. 15), the use of money or property (s. 16), any funding arrangements (s. 17) or money laundering (s. 18). The duty to disclose information (s. 19) arises where a person

(a) believes or suspects that another person has committed an offence under any of sections 15 to 18, and

(b) bases his belief or suspicion on information which comes to his attention in the course of a trade, profession, business or employment.

2 The person commits an offence if he does not disclose to a constable as soon as is reasonably practicable –

(a) his belief or suspicion, and

(b) the information on which it is based.

There is a defence for someone in employment who has used a system established by his employer for making this type of report. Although therapists are much less likely to receive this type of information than someone working in banking or financial services, it is significant that the duty to inform does cover therapists where the information is acquired 'in the course of a trade, profession, business or employment'.

Drug trafficking and money laundering

Recent developments in the law relating to the reporting of drug trafficking and money laundering for any crime have increased the obligations of people working in legal and financial services. Psychotherapists and counsellors are now less likely to acquire the kind of information that is required to be reported under the Drug Trafficking Act 1994, Proceeds of Crime Act 2002, or the Money Laundering Regulations 2007. If in doubt, seek legal advice. In many cases, disclosure of this type of information may be justified on the balance of public interest.

Statutory services and child protection

A statutory duty to report or to provide information to the authorities when requested to do so is more likely to arise when a therapist is working in association with the statutory services. Recent developments in child protection have increased many therapists' obligations with regard to the protection of children.

Where therapists know that they are working in circumstances where they have a specific obligation to pass on information, or they sense that a client is about to disclose information that could create an obligation to disclose, there is an ethical case for alerting the client to the consequences of their impending disclosure before it is made. This is most respectful of clients' autonomy and demonstrates a concern to be trustworthy and therefore is ethically desirable. However, the law does not usually require such a notice and the mere fact of disclosure having taken place is sufficient to create a legal obligation to disclose the required information, but no more than this information. Such a warning may be inappropriate if it could amount to 'tipping off' where this is forbidden, and therapists should also exercise caution before giving such a warning in any situation involving child protection, since this might in some cases adversely affect a child's welfare or compromise a child protection investigation. Obligations created by statute override the case law created by courts and are usually consistent with the requirements of Article 8 of the Human Rights Act which can be restricted by statute.

Protecting clients from self-harm and suicidal intent

Determining what is ethical and lawful when working with suicidal clients poses some of the most difficult dilemmas that are routinely encountered by therapists and mental health workers. For a discussion of the wider ethical and legal issues see Bond (2000: 96–113).

In this section we will consider whether there is a duty to breach confidentiality in order to obtain assistance for a suicidal client; whether it is legally defensible to breach confidentiality to obtain assistance; and the difference between adult and child clients in this regard. Detailed consideration of the relationship between consent and mental capacity is set out in Chapter 11.

Unlike American law, there is no general duty in England to report suicidal risk or serious self-harm. English law has a long tradition that any adult with mental capacity may refuse treatment for physical illness for good reason, irrational reasons or no reasons, even if the consequence is life threatening. This often puts doctors in a difficult position if they have a limited opportunity to give a treatment for a life-threatening medical condition but the patient is hesitating beyond the time when successful medical treatment can be given. To give treatment by force against a person's express wishes may constitute assault and other legal wrongs. Similarly if an adult client, with mental capacity, is contemplating suicide and actively forbids a therapist to seek additional help, the therapist is under a legal obligation to respect this refusal of consent. In this situation, there is no duty to breach a confidence in order to rescue the client unless working in an organisational or institutional setting such as a prison, mental health unit or other service within which there may be an obligation to protect someone from self-destruction.

The Samaritans, a confidential befriending service, provides an interesting example of how far British and Irish law permits respect of confidences, even when someone is suicidal. They assure callers that:

The Samaritans keep everything a caller says confidential unless:

- We have informed consent from a caller to pass on information
- We call an ambulance because a caller appears to be incapable of making rational decisions for him or herself
- We receive a court order requiring us to divulge information
- We are passed information about acts of terrorism or bomb warnings … (http://www.samaritans.org/about_samaritans/frequent_questions/confidential.aspx,accessed 26/09/2007)

This level of confidentiality is sustained even after a client's death.

Mere intent to kill oneself is insufficient to indicate mental illness without the existence of some other symptoms indicating an associated mental illness. The symptoms of mental illnesses such as depression, schizophrenia or a psychotic disorder might justify a referral for assessment or treatment under mental health legislation, even if this requires a limited breach of confidentiality. The Adults with Incapacity (Scotland) Act 2000 and the Mental Capacity Act 2005 set out new criteria concerning the legal capacity to give consent and when others may act on their behalf; for discussion see Chapter 11.

People under the age of 18 have a legal entitlement to privacy and confidentiality. However, the law permits the High Court to assume a greater level of responsibility to ensure the safety and welfare of children and young people until they reach adulthood and therefore it may permit life-saving treatment, for example in cases of anorexia or sickle cell anaemia. Chapter 11 explores the issues of mental capacity and of consent and confidentiality in relation to the rights of children and young people under the age of 18. From their 18th birthday onwards, a person with mental capacity is entitled to refuse treatment even when this may result in death.

The complexity of the law with regard to self-harm and suicide has resulted in therapists attempting to make the situation more manageable and to establish a right to consult with others or make a referral if the client is considered to be suicidal or at risk of serious self-harm. For example, it is widespread practice in this field to offer high levels of confidentiality except where the client poses a threat of serious harm to self or others or where the therapist is legally required to provide information. In practice, this limitation of confidentiality is used as a prior condition to receiving therapy and the therapist deems that the client has accepted it by the act of commencing therapy unless anything has been communicated to the contrary. Even though a therapist reserves the right to seek assistance for a client at risk of serious self-harm, there is still a matter of judgement about when to exercise this right and how to do so with the minimum of damage to a client's rights to privacy and confidentiality. Although this practice appears to be widespread and supported by the relevant professional bodies, we do not know of any instances where it has been considered by the courts.

Practitioners are well advised to give very careful consideration to the relevant circumstances if they are considering breaching confidentiality in order to protect an adult from self-inflicted harm, against the express wishes of that person. The balance of public interest in favour of acting is stronger where the proposed self-harm could cause physical harm to others: for example crashing a car on a public road or jumping from a height where there is the risk of causing harm to others. In other situations the therapist is legally best advised to actively seek the client's consent, whenever possible prior to obtaining additional assistance even if this involves additional time and effort, see the discussion and tables in Chapter 4.

A therapist who knows or has reasonable cause to suspect that a client is likely to harm himself or others but will not give consent for referral must carefully consider the possible consequences for their client of referral or non-referral.

With clients who have given their consent (or implied their agreement) to the counsellor acting in their best interests if they or others are at risk of harm, discuss with the client, consider and ideally discuss in supervision:

- What has the client given me permission to do?
- Does that permission include referral?

Suggestions for issues to consider if the client is unable to give consent or refuses to give consent for referral can be found at the end of the next chapter.

Making referrals

Counsellors' professional responsibility requires that they must act within the area of their personal expertise, and should consider their own limitations; see, for example, *Ethical Framework* (BACP, 2007: 5). The implication of this is that when they reach the limits of their expertise, consideration should be given to referral on where appropriate and with the client's consent. If the client does not consent to referral on, then if the client or others may be at risk of harm, the therapist should address the issues raised at the end of the next chapter.

In practice, most therapists probably would only want to make a referral without the express consent of the client in circumstances where the client had lost mental capacity, was no longer connecting with the therapist psychologically, or for any other reason was at risk of serious harm to self or others, and/or the counsellor had reached the limits of their expertise or felt that the client was in need of additional assistance or support over and above that which the counsellor alone could provide.

Being explicit with clients about confidentiality

Given that therapy is a relationship of trust, in which fidelity, beneficence and client autonomy are essential, the best way round the problem is to meet the issues head on and discuss confidentiality and its potential limitations openly with clients and to reach a mutually acceptable agreement as part of the therapeutic contract at the outset of therapy. Many therapists seem very afraid of doing this.

Some counselling organisations have a process in which there is an assessment or introductory meeting, before counselling work commences with a nominated therapist. We have been told by some of these counselling organisations that they fear that if they entered into detailed discussions about limitations on confidentiality with clients at that first meeting (which may be an assessment session), they might risk losing new clients, so at that first meeting, some may initially offer total confidentiality, leaving it to the counsellor subsequently allocated to make a different negotiation later on in the course of therapy; or they may avoid any discussion of issues of confidentiality and any possible limitations until after the first session, again leaving it to the counsellor to negotiate these issues with the client. These practices are open to potential criticism. Delay in discussion of confidentiality and failure to establish a clear agreement about it with the client at the outset of therapy may leave the client in the vulnerable position of disclosing sensitive personal confidences, with no clearly established boundaries about what will happen to that information if, for example, the client or others are at risk of serious harm. The therapist, too, is potentially vulnerable without the sound basis of explicit client consent should any further action or referral prove necessary.

We would recommend that therapists consider establishing a system in which the issue of confidentiality is discussed in a practical way at the outset with each new client, and that they make a clear agreement with the client about disclosure and referral on as part of their therapeutic contract.

A general consent condition may be agreed for the therapist to have permission to refer on if, for example, there is a 'risk of serious harm to self or others'. Agencies may interpret such a generalised permission as an adequate basis for taking positive steps to seek assistance for the person concerned unless the person actively refuses such assistance. The practical usefulness of such a condition may be that it makes a refusal of such assistance less likely, especially if the client's confidences are as well protected as the circumstances allow. However, therapists should be mindful that the existence of a widespread practice does not in itself make it lawful or immune from legal challenge. Such a general consent, if verbal and unwritten, could be interpreted in many ways and would be very difficult to substantiate and prove in a court case. A distressed client coming into counselling for an initial assessment or a first session is unlikely to recall word for word any explanation that they were given about disclosure, and their understanding of what precisely was agreed may very well be woolly and unclear. They may, for instance, be unsure as to whether a general consent to disclose actually implies or includes consent to go ahead and make a referral and to which person or agency referral would be made.

For the avoidance of doubt, it is best to discuss these issues openly and directly with the client and to agree issues of confidentiality at the outset of the therapeutic alliance, creating, wherever possible, a clear and unequivocal understanding with the client about the therapist's role and responsibilities, including those of disclosure and referral. The client will then be in the best possible position to consider issues including disclosure and referral and to give explicit and informed consent as part of the therapeutic contract. Again, legally speaking, for the avoidance of doubt, consents agreed with the client should be clearly expressed in writing, so that the client can have a copy to read through at leisure and to ensure that both the client and the therapist have a clear understanding and a record of their agreement (see Chapter 12).

Remember, however, that a client could at any time during therapy verbally or in writing withdraw their consent and then the issue of disclosure and referral would have to be revisited.

Therapists acting from self-interest

Therapists are not permitted to use information provided in confidence by clients for their own gain, for example to advance information about a potentially lucrative sale of a business or house. However, the law does recognise some legitimate self-interest as grounds for limited disclosure of information in order to protect therapists' rights. The information disclosed should be restricted to that which is necessary to achieve the permitted purpose and disclosed in confidence.

For example, therapists may disclose the information required to claim unpaid fees; defend themselves against defamatory statements; or mount a defence in a disciplinary hearing. Some therapists have been stalked or harassed by a client. Legal advice to them has usually suggested that they send a letter through a solicitor saying that if the problematic behaviour persists they will regard themselves as freed from the obligation of confidentiality in order to take reasonable preventative action. The client may be warned that any repetition of the problematic behaviour will be taken to imply consent. Any breach of confidence in such circumstances should be restricted to that which is required to protect the therapist's legitimate interests or rights. For example in a professional conduct hearing, disclosing everything known to the therapist about a client is likely to be a breach of confidence in both ethics and law, whereas restricting disclosures to those that relate to the accusations under consideration would be legally defensible.

No advance warning to clients is required if the therapist is concerned that the client is about to commit a serious crime against the therapist. A breach of confidence that is restricted to the information required in order to obtain assistance is legally defensible, for example in stalking where the risk is protracted. Concern about confidentiality ought not to delay the seeking of appropriate assistance where there is a real risk of serious harm or a serious crime being committed against the therapist. Some therapists have suffered serious physical assault and, exceptionally, some have been murdered.

Possible outcomes of litigation for breach of confidentiality

The courts do take violations of someone's confidences or privacy very seriously. A court may:

- Impose a court order in order to prevent a breach of confidence, if the possibility of this occurring is known in advance.
- Award damages to compensate someone for their losses and harm arising from the breach.
- Award aggravated or exemplary damages which go beyond that required for mere compensation in order to show judicial disapproval of the behaviour of someone who has breached confidentiality (this does not apply in Scotland).

Imprisonment has been threatened as a possible consequence of breach of confidentiality. In a case that occurred at the height of the moral panic over HIV and AIDS, a judge speculated that imprisonment could be an appropriate penalty if any health workers were ever identified who had informed the press about the identities of doctors diagnosed with AIDS (*X* v. *Y* [1988]).

In some situations, clients may prefer to pursue action for breach of confidence under data protection legislation (see Chapter 6) or a complaint for breach of professional conduct with the applicable professional body. Both these courses of action will usually expose the client to a lower level of financial risk than a court case where they could be required to invest large sums of money and face the possibility of paying the other side's costs if the case is lost.

Significance of consent

The best solutions to issues concerning confidentiality will nearly always be disclosures made with the client's consent. Consent provides the best protection of everyone's interests and is worth the investment of time and effort. However, the law concerning consent is quite complex because of the different possible circumstances and mental capacity of the person giving consent. Under recent developments in statutory law, there are distinctions between an adult who has mental capacity and one who does not (see the Glossary and Chapter 11 for definitions and discussion). The law also distinguishes between adults and children concerning consent. As consent is so critical to the management of both confidentiality and record keeping, we have devoted Chapter 11 to this topic.

4 Responding to Dilemmas over Confidentiality

I am not sure how to apply general legal principles to the dilemmas that I sometimes encounter in my work with clients.

My heart sinks when a client starts to raise issues where I might need to break their confidentiality. I don't imagine that I will ever feel comfortable breaking a confidence but it would help if I was surer of my grounds for doing so … Sometimes keeping confidences is a burden too. I am holding information that causes me to feel anxious but I can do nothing with it. I am left hoping that I am doing the right thing and watching how things work out.

It's the nature of a dilemma. You feel damned if you do and damned if you don't. It's a dilemma because it isn't clear what to do for the best. Legal dilemmas are particularly tricky because I have to look beyond my area of expertise.

In the previous chapter we took a wide-ranging overview of the law concerning confidentiality and privacy and how it applies to therapists' responsibilities. As we worked on this chapter we became aware that a number of dilemmas are experienced with sufficient frequency to require some specific guidance. In this chapter we have provided a summary of these issues and directed attention to the relevant law. We start by considering circumstances in which the client is considered to be at risk of inflicting harm on others, before considering situations where the client is considered to be inflicting harm on self. The final section considers situations in which children and young people are vulnerable to abuse. The chapter closes with a series of questions to be considered in any challenging dilemma over confidentiality.

A client at risk of harming others

An acute ethical dilemma for therapists arises when clients threaten significant harm to others or reveal that they are actively involved in serious crime that harms others or the community. Clients who attempt to insist on confidentiality in these circumstances are asking for a degree of respect to be shown for their own rights that they are unwilling to show to others. The therapist may experience this as a question of personal and professional integrity over how far they are willing to be morally implicated in the client's actions. The law takes a less personalised approach by directing attention to where the balance of the public interest lies and the existence of any legal duties. Please refer to table 4.1 below.

Table 4.1   Deciding whether to breach confidentiality to prevent clients harming others

Situation	Breaching confidentiality	Legal authorities
Preventing or assisting the detection of terrorism	There is a duty to disclose specified types of information acquired in the course of a trade, profession, business or employment: see Chapter 3.	Section 19 and s 38B of the Terrorism Act 2000.
Preventing or assisting detection of drug trafficking and money laundering	Respond in the same way as for any serious crime. Requirements to report, which included therapists in the past, have largely been replaced in current UK legislation: see Chapter 3.	Drug Trafficking Act 1994. Proceeds of Crime Act 2002.
Prevention of serious crime	Permissible at discretion of therapist acting in good faith to notify authorities.	In common law, the public interest in the prevention and detection of serious crime is greater than in protecting confidences.
	A court will not impose any penalties for breach of confidence that is considered to be in the public interest. Such breaches are 'defensible'.	Balance of public interest in common law.
	A client cannot insist on confidentiality over serious crime.	Law of equity under the principle that 'there is no confidence in iniquity'.
Prevention of serious physical harm likely to be inflicted by client on another adult	A breach of confidence is defensible in order to protect someone from serious physical harm inflicted by a client where the information is given in good faith, reasonably well founded, restricted to that necessary to prevent the harm, and communicated in confidence to either the authorities or the intended victim	Common law – balance of public interest. Where a client is likely to harm another of the therapist's clients, failure to act to protect the victim may amount to negligence. Legal advice should be sought if circumstances permit this. In an emergency situation, it may be better to avert a serious and real risk of harm by warning the potential victim, if they are unaware of the danger, or informing police to prevent immediate injury. This type of dilemma may arise when providing couple counselling while also working with one of them individually.

Table 4.1   (Continued)

Situation	Breaching confidentiality	Legal authorities
		The ethical issues are increased when seeing a client who is intending to inflict harm on another person who is also your client, without one or both clients knowing that the other is receiving therapy from you. Consider issues in the Disclosure Checklist on page 99.
Prevention of psychological harm likely to be inflicted by client on another adult	No general grounds to breach confidentiality.	Common law balance of public interest requires prevention of serious *physical* harm. However, the law is moving towards taking substantial psychological harm more seriously, especially if this harm amounts to psychiatric illness or is being inflicted on a vulnerable adult. The law provides protection against stalking, harassment and discrimination in many circumstances but it is less clear whether these situations would justify a breach of confidence. Work with the client's consent or seek legal advice.
Knowledge of significant harm being caused or likely to be caused to a child/young person		See Table 4.3 later in this chapter.
Prevention of serious physical harm being inflicted by client on self, whether life threatening or not, *that places others at risk of serious physical harm*	Respond as though for prevention of serious crime where crime might result or on the balance of public interest to prevent serious physical harm to others.	Balance of public interest. Consider the issues in the Disclosure Checklist (p. 99).
Prevention of self-inflicted serious physical harm to an adult client	May be defensible to consult a medic or specialist in mental health on a confidential basis to investigate the possibility of compulsory assessment or treatment *where mental illness is suspected*.	No case law could be discovered but may be defensible on the balance of public interest – depending on the circumstances. Consider the issues in the Disclosure Checklist (p. 99).
	If the client explicitly refuses permission to seek medical assistance for the treatment of physical injuries.	Check that client has mental capacity. No general right to breach confidentiality against the express wishes of the client. Persuasion to

(Continued)

Table 4.1 (Continued)

Situation	Breaching confidentiality	Legal authorities
		accept help is legally safer. Adults with mental capacity may refuse treatments for physical illnesses or offers of assistance even if it seems contrary to their best interests or unreasonable. (*St George's Healthcare NHS Trust v S* [1999])
Prevention of self-inflicted serious physical harm by someone under the age of 18	There is no general legal requirement to breach confidentiality but therapists working in public authorities or associated organisations may be obliged to do so under child protection law and their contract of employment. All therapists should comply with child protection law.	The public policy and the balance of public interest in common law favours ensuring that children are protected and therefore would protect a breach of confidence, even against the young person's express wishes to obtain assistance or advice. Consider the issues in the Disclosure Checklist (p. 99).
Seeking treatment for minor or superficial self-inflicted harm by someone between 16 and 18 years old	The express wishes of the person concerned should normally be respected, however, mental capacity should be carefully considered along with the issues on the Disclosure Checklist (p. 99).	Family Law Reform Act 1969; Age of Legal Capacity (Scotland) Act 1991.
Seeking treatment for minor or superficial self-inflicted harm by someone under 16	The express wishes of someone who is 'Gillick competent' i.e. having sufficient age, intelligence and understanding to understand the consequences of declining treatment should normally be respected. However, consider the issues in the Disclosure Checklist (p. 99).	*Gillick v West Norfolk and Wisbech Area Health Authority* [1985]; Age of Legal Capacity (Scotland) Act 1991.
	Where someone lacks the mental capacity to give consent, consider seeking the involvement and consent of someone with parental responsibility. (One person's consent is sufficient if there is more than one person with parental responsibility.) Whilst the young person's wishes and feelings should be taken into account, their welfare should be paramount and guide any further action.	Lord Fraser's judgment in Gillick case (see above).

Clients at risk of harm to themselves

In Table 4.2 we consider different situations that are likely to be encountered by therapists in which clients are considered to be at serious risk of harming themselves. This guidance relates to situations where there is no prior agreement that a therapist may seek assistance for a client, even if this means breaching confidentiality, or the client is refusing to permit a referral. As always, the best way of resolving difficulties over confidentiality is with the client's consent whenever possible.

Abuse of children

The legal framework concerning the protection of children and young people has undergone several substantial changes in recent years. There is now greater emphasis on hearing 'the voice of the child' and in the context of child care legislation, children and young people are able to participate more fully in court proceedings about them and in decisions made about their care.

At the same time, as a result of some significant failures in the child care and protection system, new measures are being developed in England and Scotland to encourage and facilitate better inter-agency co-operation and information sharing in child protection work; this is discussed further in Chapter 9.

As children's circumstances differ, each decision is case specific, and therapists working in this field need a sound knowledge of relevant law, ethics and government guidance to provide the framework within which these difficult decisions are made. Table 4.3 covers some of the issues which practitioners have found helpful to consider in their decision making. Further information, guidance and resources can be found later in this chapter, in Chapters 9, 11 and 12 and in the References and further reading at the end of the book.

Failure to comply with child protection law and procedures (when under an obligation to do so) that resulted in further harm to a child client could lead to that child potentially having a legal claim against the therapist in the future, perhaps surfacing many years later. Legal liability might arise in negligence or breach of contract but is not restricted to these. This would not apply where the young person concerned was over 16 with sufficient mental capacity to be considered Gillick competent and had explicitly refused their consent to disclosure.

Therapists working in local authorities, health services and any other agencies or organisations regulated by child protection legislation have a duty to comply with the child protection procedures set out in Part 1 of *Working Together to Safeguard Children: A guide to Inter-Agency Working to Safeguard and Promote the Welfare of Children* (DfES, 2006c). Therapists in private practice should be aware of these provisions and also refer to *What to do if you are worried that a child is being abused* (DfES, 2006a).

Therapists employed by non-government agencies or organisations may have an obligation to report under their contract of employment. It is increasingly common

Table 4.2   Deciding whether to breach confidentiality to protect clients at risk of harm to themselves

In all these situations it may be helpful to consider the issues in the Disclosure Checklist (at page 99), in supervision, and where appropriate, with advice and with the client.

Situation	Breaching confidentiality	Legal authorities
Prevention of serious physical harm being inflicted by client on self, whether life threatening or not, *that places others at risk of serious physical harm*	Respond as though for prevention of serious crime where crime might result or on the balance of public interest to prevent serious physical harm to others.	Balance of public interest.
Prevention of self-inflicted serious physical harm to an *adult* client *where the harm is restricted to that person*	May be defensible to consult a medic or specialist in mental health on a confidential basis to investigate the possibility of compulsory assessment or treatment *where mental illness is suspected* or where mental capacity is an issue.	No case law could be discovered but may be defensible on the balance of public interest – depending on the circumstances.
	If the client explicitly refuses permission to seek medical assistance for the treatment of physical injuries. Check mental capacity – is the client's ability to think clearly affected by the injuries?	No general right to breach confidentiality against the express wishes of the client. Persuasion to accept help is legally safer. Adults may refuse treatments for physical illnesses or offers of assistance even if it seems contrary to their best interests or unreasonable (*St George's Healthcare NHS Trust v S* [1999]).
Prevention of self-inflicted serious physical harm by someone over the age of 16 but under the age of 18	Young people over 16 are treated as adults regarding consent, but are still subject to child protection legislation and to the authority of the High Court/Court of Session.	The public policy and the balance of public interest in common law favours child protection. In situations of sufficient seriousness, the balance of public interest would protect a breach to obtain professional assistance or advice in confidence, even against the young person's express wishes.
	There is no general legal requirement to breach confidentiality but therapists working in public authorities or associated organisations may be obliged to do so under child protection law and their contract of employment. See Chapter 11, and if necessary seek legal advice.	The High Court/Court of Session may sanction life-saving treatment against a young person's express wishes.

(Continued)

Table 4.2   (Continued)

Situation	Breaching confidentiality	Legal authorities
Seeking treatment for minor or superficial self-inflicted harm by someone between 16 and 18 years old	The express wishes of the person concerned should normally be respected, but consider mental capacity and the Disclosure Checklist, see page 99.	Family Law Reform Act 1969.
Seeking treatment for minor or superficial self-inflicted harm by someone under 16	The express wishes of someone who is 'Gillick competent' i.e. having sufficient age, intelligence and understanding to understand the consequences of declining treatment should normally be respected.	*Gillick v West Norfolk and Wisbech Area Health Authority* [1985].
	Where a young person lacks the capacity to give consent, consider seeking the involvement and consent of someone with parental responsibility for them, and if more than one, the consent of one person with parental responsibility will suffice. Whilst the young person's wishes and feelings should be taken into account, their welfare should be paramount and guide any further action.	Lord Fraser's judgment in the above case.

for any funding from health and social services to require that workers comply with the procedures applicable to organisations regulated by child protection legislation.

The legal obligations of a therapist working outside organisations covered by child protection legislation are less clear, but therapists in private practice working with children and families are well advised to develop and implement a child protection policy which complies with current child protection procedures.

Current law has moved in the direction of enabling professionals to share information about vulnerable children and adults so that they can be better protected. It has also strengthened the requirements for many professionals to actively share information on a confidential basis. This follows thirty years of inquiries into the deaths of children caused by neglect and abuse in which it emerged that several professionals were concerned about the child but only knew about a small part of the total circumstances. It seemed that each professional held one or two pieces of the jigsaw sufficient to cause concern but no one held sufficient pieces to make the entire picture from which the full danger to the person concerned was apparent:

Table 4.3   Issues to be considered when someone discloses abuse of children

In all cases where there is any child protection concern, discuss the issues in supervision, and seek additional advice, e.g. from lawyers or social services where necessary. See Chapters 9, 11 and 12, and *Guidance: What to do if you are worried that a child is being abused* (DfES, 2006a); *Information Sharing – A Practitioner's Guide* (DfES, 2006b); *Working Together to Safeguard Children: A guide to Inter-Agency Working to Safeguard and Promote the Welfare of Children* (DfES, 2006c), and *Confidentiality: Protecting and Providing Information* (GMC, *2004*). These and other useful guidance documents are listed in the References at the end of the book.

Type of disclosure	Issues to be considered
An adult who discloses that they have abused children in the past	<ul><li>Are they likely to do this again?</li><li>Are there children at imminent risk from them now?</li><li>Are the authorities aware of this past abuse already?</li><li>This is a serious crime – see above.</li></ul>
An adult who admits to causing any present harm or is likely to cause any future harm to a child e.g. sexual, physical, emotional or through neglect	<ul><li>What is the harm that this person admits to causing?</li><li>Are the authorities aware of this situation already?</li><li>If the person is an active paedophile, then children may be actually suffering significant harm now and may be at risk in the future.</li><li>Child sexual abuse constitutes grounds for an inquiry by social services and is potentially a serious crime – see above.</li><li>Causing any harm (e.g. physical, emotional or through neglect) to a child is also potentially criminal and in any event may constitute grounds for an investigation by social services.</li></ul>
Young person over 16 with mental capacity or 'Gillick competent' child tells you of abuse they suffered in the past or are suffering now	If they refuse their explicit consent to disclose, their decision should be respected, but … <ul><li>Ask yourself, why are they telling you this, now, as a trusted adult?</li><li>Bear in mind that other children in the family/neighbourhood may be at risk.</li><li>Wherever possible, especially if other children are at risk, persuade the child to allow you to refer with their consent, and support the child through the subsequent process.</li><li>If the child refuses consent for disclosure, then you have to weigh up client's wishes versus public interest – and whether to breach without client consent and to be able to justify that decision.</li></ul>
Child under 16 and who is *not* 'Gillick competent', tells you of abuse they suffered in the past or are suffering now	<ul><li>Ask yourself, why are they telling you this, now, as a trusted adult?</li><li>They do not have legal capacity to refuse consent to disclose/refer.</li><li>The child victim may have suffered significant harm and also be at risk of future harm.</li><li>Government agencies and health authorities have a duty to protect the child and act in the public interest.</li></ul>

Table 4.3   (Continued)

Type of disclosure	Issues to be considered
	• Local authorities have a duty to investigate and to provide help and protection for children under the age of 18 in need or at risk of significant harm (Children Act 1989, Children Act 2004, Children (Scotland) Act 1995). • Act in accordance with current child protection law and procedures, see *What to do if you are worried that a child is being abused* (DfES, 2006a) and *Working Together to Safeguard Children* (DfES, 2006c). • Bear in mind that other children in the family/neighbourhood may be at risk. • Not only child protection issues here but also potentially serious crime. • No duty to tell those with parental responsibility if to tell them might put this child or other children at risk of further abuse or if they are the alleged abusers. Under child protection procedures, social services would conduct an investigation (in certain cases jointly with the police) and they will handle any necessary communication with those with parental responsibility.
Young person under the age of 18 or a younger child admits to causing significant harm to another child	• Ask yourself, why are they telling you this, now, as a trusted adult? • The child causing the harm may themselves be in need of help as well as the child victim. • The child victim may have suffered significant harm and also be at risk of future harm. • Local authorities are under a duty to provide help and protection for children under the age of 18 (Children Act 1989 s 17, Children (Scotland) Act 1995). • Local authorities are under a duty to investigate where there is a risk of significant harm to a child. • Act in accordance with current child protection law and procedures. See *What to do if you are worried that a child is being abused* (DfES, 2006a) and *Working Together to Safeguard Children* (DfES, 2006c). • Bear in mind that other children in the family/neighbourhood may be at risk.

see *Beyond Blame* (Reder, Duncan et al., 1994). The tipping point which led to the Children Act 2004 and the development of new policy and practice in Every Child Matters has been the tragic death of Victoria Climbié in February 2000.

Victoria spent much of her last days, in the winter of 1999–2000, living and sleeping in a bath in an unheated bathroom, bound hand and foot inside a bin bag, lying in her own urine and faeces. It is not surprising then that towards the end of her short life, Victoria was stooped like an old lady and could walk only with great difficulty. (Lord Laming, 2003)

Lord Laming's report revealed both the ways in which determined abusers can seek to hide from the authorities and a catalogue of poor practice by those responsible for child protection and the care of vulnerable children. It also reveals how inadequate protection systems compound the difficulties for any vulnerable person asking for help to escape abuse. Gradually, since the Children Act 1989, which provides that the child's wishes and feelings should be taken into account, more attention has been paid to listening to children and taking what they say seriously. Despite this, some children still remain unheard and opportunities should be readily available for children seeking help to speak with professionals and trusted adults. Teachers, doctors and other professionals, including counsellors, may be the first recipients of a child's disclosure of abuse or neglect. Victoria Climbié never got as far as seeing a counsellor. It is salutary to ask ourselves how we as therapists would respond in a similar situation in judging the balance between respecting privacy and confidentiality and the dangers to the child concerned or the balance between the rights of adult 'carers' and the child. Children's services are currently being restructured as a result of the Laming Report. As a consequence, more therapists may become involved in working for the new services or alongside them.

We are only too aware, from our personal practice and from what other therapists have told us, that many who consider making a referral of a child or a vulnerable adult to social services or other helping agencies hesitate to do so. They are stopped from acting partially because of concern to protect their client's privacy and from respect for what has been disclosed in confidence but also because they have had experience of, or have heard from others about, situations where the system appears to have failed. In the worst cases, it may have left the young person more vulnerable to further abuse and destroyed the therapeutic relationship so that even that support is lost. What we have to ask ourselves is whether this fear really constitutes a reason not to refer. Why is the child telling us about the abuse they suffer? Are they telling us as a trusted adult now because they actually want and need help, but are afraid? As therapists, we must remember that we have only our client's perspective of the situation and therefore we often do not know the wider picture. In addition, we may not have specialist training and experience in child protection and so there may be many factors of which we are unaware. If we refer a client on, for example within the child protection framework, we are placing that child within the care of a team of professionals, who together have a much wider body of shared experience and expertise and access to resources than we have, and who have the ability to investigate the bigger picture and act appropriately to protect the client's welfare. Recent developments in services may mean that we as therapists can become part of that team, continuing to support clients through the protective process, and do our best to make sure that it works for them. It may be that as a profession we need to develop collective strategies through our professional bodies to monitor our experiences of the new services and to participate at a collective level to remedy any deficiencies. It may not be the legal framework that is failing vulnerable people but the adequacy of systems and practice. This is another theme to emerge from the Laming Report.

All therapists should familiarise themselves with the current government guidance, *What to do if you are worried that a child is being abused* (DfES, 2006a). Those working within the NHS should also refer to *Confidentiality: NHS Code of Practice* (DH, 2003a). Therapists working in England can find statutory and non-statutory guidance on inter-agency collaboration in *Working Together to Safeguard Children: A guide to Inter-Agency Working to Safeguard and Promote the Welfare of Children* (DfES, 2006c) and *Information Sharing – A Practitioner's Guide* (DfES, 2006b), available through the strategic programme Every Child Matters. The general principles of this guidance apply across England although names of agencies and roles may vary across the different local authorities.

Further resources providing information on child protection, the Children Act 1989, the Children Act 2004 and child protection in Scotland are included at the end of this book.

Issues to be considered during dilemmas over confidentiality

With all clients, including those who have refused consent, discuss with the client if appropriate, consider and ideally also discuss in supervision these issues:

- What is the likelihood of serious harm in this case?
- Is this serious harm imminent?
- If I refer, what is likely to happen?
- If I do not refer, what is likely to happen?
- Do the likely consequences of non-referral include any serious harm to the client or others?
- If so, are the likely consequences of non-referral preventable?
- What would have to happen to prevent serious harm to client or others?
- Is there anything I (or anyone else) can do to assist in preventing this harm to my client or others?
- What steps would need to be taken to implement such assistance?
- How could the client be helped to accept assistance/the proposed action?
- Does my client have the mental capacity to give explicit informed consent (or refusal of consent) at this moment in time?
- If the client does not have mental capacity, then what are my professional responsibilities to the client and in the public interest?
- If the client has mental capacity, but does not consent to my proposed action (e.g. referral to a GP), what would be my legal and professional situation if I went ahead and did it anyway?

Further guidance on issues of consent and mental capacity can be found in Chapter 11.

5 Confidentiality in Supervision, Training, Research and Audit

There is a strong benefit to clients and to the public in ensuring that therapists are competent and are working to an adequate standard. Supervision, training, research and audit of services make significant contributions to advancing and protecting competence and adequate standards. However, many clients are probably completely unaware of this professional infrastructure that operates outside their view. We are aware that some therapists take the view that the beneficial purpose of these activities and the professional culture of confidentiality justifies them in their decision not to trouble clients with unnecessary concerns. Others have decided that it is more respectful of clients if they are made aware of this infrastructure of professional support. In this chapter we will ask what should clients be told and how should their views be taken into account to satisfy the legal requirements of confidentiality?

We will start with supervision because it is the role perhaps least understood by non-therapists. It may also be the role where practice is most likely to lag behind current legal requirements.

Supervision

I only tell my clients about my supervision arrangements if they ask. They never do … well almost never do … unless they know how we work.

I have wondered if I should be routinely telling my clients about my supervision arrangements and the name of my supervisor. But I am reluctant to add another thing that could delay the start of counselling … especially for my more desperate clients.

I don't tell my supervisor anything more than the first name of my client so she doesn't ever know who they are. Even if she did think she knew someone, she is bound by confidentiality, just like I am.

No. I don't say anything about supervision. Most of my clients come for work-related problems where there is no tradition of supervision for workers doing work that is, frankly, often more stressful and unpleasant than being a therapist. They would not understand and if they did … I am afraid they would be envious. Either way, it's a complication I could do without.

The information that goes to all clients mentions that we have supervision. But it doesn't say more than that. No client has ever asked me about it.

I make a point of choosing supervisors who are completely independent of where I offer therapy. It really helps to have someone looking at things with fresh eyes. She notices things that I take for granted. Sometimes, it makes all the difference in helping the client.

This last quotation from an experienced therapist highlights the benefits of supervision for clients and provides a justification for supervision that that has long been recognised (Bond, 1990; Proctor, 1986). However, the role of supervision as part of the infrastructure of activities that supports most therapists in the UK is probably little understood by the public and lawyers. In everyday use, supervision suggests an activity undertaken by someone with greater expertise and/or managerial responsibility for the work of the person being supervised. This is not usually the case in therapy.

Within therapy there are two different uses of the term 'supervision', neither of which exactly fits this general understanding of the role. In the psychoanalytic tradition and in most therapeutic approaches in the USA, supervision is largely restricted to supporting trainees who, on completion of their training, may work unsupervised. In this type of trainee supervision, the supervisor assumes both a greater degree of expertise and some responsibility for overseeing the therapy with a client. This is reasonably close to the widespread understanding of supervision. However, in Britain there is a tradition of independent supervision which continues throughout the training and the working life of many therapists. In this approach, the supervisor is regarded as an independent facilitator who helps the therapist examine their practice and consider any challenges that arise. Typically there is limited or no direct accountability for the work undertaken by the therapist as supervisor because the role of the supervisor operates largely outside any line management accountability and is probably best understood as acting as a professional mentor.

The situation is further complicated because requirements for supervision vary between professional bodies. Both BACP and the BPS Division of Counselling Psychology require that their practitioner members receive regular and ongoing supervision (BACP, 2007: 6 section 26; BPS, 2005). Both professional bodies emphasise the importance of distinguishing and separating the supervisory relationship from any line management (BACP, 2007: 6 section 26; BPS, 2005 section 2.1). This separation of line management from supervisory functions is not widely understood outside these professional bodies. UKCP has no general requirement for supervision although some sections and groups within UKCP have adopted a requirement to have independent supervision on a similar basis to other national bodies.

The use of supervision and supportive consultations about work with clients carries significant legal implications with regard to confidentiality and safeguards for client privacy. The ethical emphasis on the supervisor being independent of any managerial responsibility for the therapy has the effect of widening the circle of confidentiality in ways that may surprise many clients if it is kept invisible to them. In this section, we consider the management of this extension of confidentiality where clients' identities are disclosed or withheld in consultations between the therapist and supervisor. In both cases, we assume that the supervisor is bound to confidentiality about client-related information. This is normal practice within therapy both for supervision required by professional bodies and for informal consultations with any professional to assist the delivery of therapy to a specific client. The law of confidentiality applies equally to formal supervision and informal consultations concerning specific clients. Issues of confidentiality do not arise if the consultation is about working with a general class of people or around an issue that is not linked to a specific person. So if the therapist is asking for general guidance about working with people affected by depression or addiction, there are no issues of confidentiality until either the person being consulted or the therapist makes reference to work with specific clients.

Supervision where clients' identities are disclosed or may be discovered from details disclosed about them

Some therapists and supervisors prefer to discuss named clients because it reduces the possibility of confusion between cases and helps to prevent any conflict of interests emerging as the case unfolds. For example, when names are used, the supervisor is able to declare prior knowledge of the client or a potential conflict of interest before the details of the therapy are disclosed. The original supervisor might decline to hear anything further and an alternative supervisor might be sought in such circumstances.

Other therapists prefer to strictly restrict the information they disclose in supervision that might identify their clients, for example by using only first names and withholding non-essential information that might identify a client. This practice is a compromise between identifying clients and fully protecting their identity. However, the law of confidentiality and privacy does apply to communications where the client's identity can be deduced from either the distinctive features of the case or the recipient's prior knowledge of the person concerned. When this occurs, the legal responsibilities and potential liabilities for breach of confidence are the same as when the client has been named.

From a legal point of view, the communication of private information about an identifiable person constitutes a breach of confidence. It ceases to be a breach of confidence where the client has given consent. The optimum practice is that the client should have given her prior consent on the basis of knowing to whom information will be disclosed, the purpose of the disclosure, the type of information to be disclosed and the likely outcomes of any disclosure. This consent can be sought prior to starting the therapy or may be established during therapy prior to discussion in supervision. Implicit consent is probably legally sufficient for an oral discussion in supervision. To satisfy the requirements of implicit consent, the client should have been informed that the therapy may be discussed in supervision and not taken the opportunity to object. (Written communications or sharing written information such as showing a case file could be subject to data protection requirements and therefore would require explicit consent: see Chapter 6.) A client's refusal to allow disclosure in supervision ought to be respected. However, a therapist is not obliged to offer therapy without supervision and some will be reluctant to do so.

Supervision where the client's identity is withheld or disguised

Some therapists seek to protect their clients from being identified in supervision by only discussing them anonymously (by withholding their identity), or pseudonymously (by substituting a fictitious identity, typically a false name). To prevent a breach of confidence, the protection of the client's identity must be sufficient to prevent the client's identity being deduced, even by somebody who has knowledge of that person. For example, the supervisor may have met the client socially and learned some details of her life without the therapist knowing of these encounters. Avoiding any possibility of someone deducing a client's identity is a very high standard of anonymity. If such a standard could be achieved, would it be sufficient in law to avoid the charge of a breach of confidentiality or privacy? There is no straightforward and completely secure answer to this question.

The Court of Appeal in England has controversially upheld that thoroughly anonymised information does not constitute a breach of confidentiality or privacy in *R. v. Department of Health, ex parte Source Informatics Ltd* [2001]. The company, Source Informatics, was challenging Department of Health Guidance that doctors and pharmacists ought to cease providing them with information. The company bought details of prescriptions from doctors and pharmacists for modest payments. The identity of patients was not included so the data was anonymous and did not compromise patient confidentiality. It did include the date, details of the prescribed product, and the doctor's name. This information was sold by Source Informatics to pharmaceutical companies who used it for market research. The Department of Health Guidance had stated that anonymised information did not remove the duty of confidence owed to patients. As no provision had been made for obtaining patient consent, nor could consent be implied as patients were unaware of the practice and had no opportunity to object, the Guidance concluded that there were no legitimate grounds to justify the breach of confidence. The company sought to challenge this interpretation of the law.

The Court of Appeal found in favour of the company. On the assumption that other courts follow this judgment, the disclosure of anonymous information is permissible provided that:

1   An acceptable level of anonymity has been achieved so that the risk of the client being identified from the data disclosed is remote. Merely removing or changing the name of a client would be insufficient if the client is described in detail or unusual characteristics about the client have been disclosed, and
2   There is no gain to the therapist that would compromise the therapist's undivided loyalty to the client, nor would a therapist's actions be considered unconscionable, a controversial test applied in this case based on the longstanding law of equity, and
3   The client has not objected to or forbidden disclosure of even anonymous information.

The Scottish courts would not be bound to follow this judgment, though are likely to attach weight to it if considering the same issues. There are two issues that therapists ought to bear in mind before relying too heavily on the decision in the Source Informatics case. First, disclosures in supervision about clients are made within free-flowing and open-ended discussion in which it is difficult to pre-determine and control exactly what will be disclosed. This is rather different from the level of control to protect privacy that can be exercised over predictable types of information disclosed on the fixed format of the prescription. It is possible and indeed probable that there are significant differences in fact between the circumstances of disclosure in Source Informatics and the methods of disclosure in supervision. Secondly, the legal reasoning in the Source Informatics case is much criticised as being based on too narrow an interpretation of privacy. The critics of the decision argue that privacy is not restricted to protecting someone's identity but, on a wider interpretation, privacy concerns someone's dignity, rights to autonomy and control over the use of private information. If a future case adopted this wider application of privacy, which would be consistent with the gradual introduction of the full weight of human rights, then a client's right to anonymised information about themselves would be strengthened. Many legal commentators question the narrowness of the interpretation of privacy in the Source Informatics case and thus question its reliability as a general guide to current law (Jackson, 2006: 349–351; Mason & Laurie, 2006: 279–280; Pattenden, 2003: 147–150; Pattinson, 2006: 199–204). Thus it is legally and ethically safer to obtain a client's consent for discussions about them in supervision. Where this is not practicable it may be permissible to rely on implied consent, provided the client is aware that the therapy will be discussed in supervision, has been given the opportunity to object and has not objected.

If therapists wish to rely on the principle that anonymised information cannot constitute a breach of confidence, they should challenge themselves with a controversial test used in the Source Informatics derived from the principles of equity. This test is known as the 'troubled conscience test'. It asks whether 'a reasonable therapist's conscience ought to be troubled by the proposed use of information about clients'. If the answer is 'yes' then it is better to work on the basis of consent.

The BPS Division for Counselling Psychology favours managing issues of confidentiality and privacy in supervision through client consent: 'Practitioners will … inform clients of issues of confidentiality including those pertaining to … supervision … during the contracting process' (BPS, 2005). Given the complexity and uncertainty of some aspects of the law, this appears to be sound advice.

Training

I feel quite torn between working on my vulnerability to improve myself as a therapist and hiding my vulnerable bits from being known by my trainers, assessors, institute and perhaps even my professional body. Unlike in my own therapy, I think it is quite easy to lose control of private information as a trainee.

As a tutor, I feel like a spider catching clients' and trainees' secrets and mostly keeping them in my net but just occasionally, when I am sufficiently concerned about protecting clients, passing them on to another web or even a network of webs.

I consider that what I model as trainer is a powerful and perhaps the most powerful influence on trainees' future practice. I like to be as conscientious about managing their confidences on the basis of consent as I hope they will be with their clients.

In this section, we will consider disclosure of information about clients during training as well as personal information about trainees, particularly as part of their assessment.

Information about work with clients may flow in many different directions during training. Trainers may disclose details of work with their own clients as examples to educate their students. Trainee therapists may disclose details of their work with their clients to trainers in ways that are very similar to supervision. This information may be communicated on a one to one basis with a tutor, which is least intrusive on the client's privacy, or in discussions in seminar groups or whole classes where the client's privacy is less easily protected. For the reasons given in the section on supervision, these types of activity require implied consent as a minimum standard. Implied consent requires that the client knows that the therapist is receiving training and may present part or all the work with the client on an anonymous or named basis, whichever is the case, and that the client has not objected. The case for explicit consent as the norm in these circumstances is considerably stronger because of the potentially larger numbers of people involved, both as students and staff. Even where the discussions are on an anonymous basis, the risk of someone inferring the identity of the client is increased. A further protection for the client is to ensure that all recipients of client information are themselves bound by confidentiality.

In addition to oral presentations, training frequently requires written analysis, presented as case studies about therapy with selected clients. Usual practice is to:

- Avoid disclosing the identity of the client by anonymising or disguising the identity,
- Obtain the client's consent in advance, and
- Bind the recipients of the information to confidentiality concerning the client.

Where all of these conditions are implemented, the requirements of the law concerning confidentiality, privacy and data protection are being adequately observed.

So far we have been concentrating on the clients' rights to confidentiality. But what are the rights of students with regard to information about themselves? During the course of their training, students may choose to or be required to disclose personally sensitive information about themselves. Normal practice is to establish an understanding between students, their tutors, assessors and examiners that personally sensitive information may be disclosed in order to ensure a properly conducted and fair assessment. Even when students have not explicitly agreed to this, they may be taken to have given implied consent if they have not explicitly objected and have continued to submit work for assessment. Where a student refuses to allow a communication of information that is deemed essential for their assessment, there are broadly two possible outcomes. One option is that the work is withheld and deemed not to have been submitted, with the result that the rules of the course concerning non-submission of work would apply. However, let us suppose that the staff responsible for the assessment of the student have grounds for believing that the work contains indications of some serious weaknesses that could put future clients at significant risk of harm. Are these circumstances in which it would be legally right to override the student's objections?

The answer depends on deciding the balance between public and private interests informed by case law and the Human Rights Act 1998. The public interest is in securing an adequately competent profession and ensuring the avoidance of harm caused by members of that profession, especially if those sources of harm could have been identified and remedied, or prevented. These public interests are incompatible with the private interests of the student who wishes to use confidentiality as a shield to avoid proper assessment of his submitted work or disclosure of personally sensitive information acquired about him. There are no reported cases to guide anyone here but the decision and actions that follow would need to be proportional to the perceived risk in order to satisfy the proportionality test required by human rights. In *Sporrong* v. *Sweden* [1982] this test was defined as the balance between 'the demands of the general interest of the community and the requirements for the protection of the individual's fundamental rights'. This test was later developed in *R.* v. *Secretary of State for the Home Department, exparte Daly* [2001] into three stages. These require a court to satisfy itself that that the objective is sufficiently important to justify limiting a fundamental right; there is a rational link between the measures taken and the objective; and the means used to impair the right are no more than is necessary to accomplish the objective.

The student's right to confidentiality about personally sensitive information (see next chapter) should be protected throughout the assessment process, and those involved in receiving information should be correspondingly bound by confidentiality. Assessment procedures typically require written assessments by tutors and examiners and the minutes of meetings. The student concerned will usually be able to use their rights under the Data Protection Act 1998 to gain access to those records where they relate directly to him or her.

If the level of concern about a student is such that the educational institution wishes to inform relevant professional bodies or a student's employer, this extends the communication of confidential information in ways that will probably have consequences for the student in curtailing career opportunities and loss of income. It is not a decision to be taken lightly because, if the decision to widen the scope of disclosure is legally unjustified, there is the possibility of large damages being claimed against the training provider by the student for future loss of earnings. The contrast between the requirements for regulated professions like medicine and unregulated professions like counselling, psychotherapy and most applied psychology is stark. Statutory regulation of doctors is undertaken by a legally authorised body, currently the General Medical Council, where procedures tend to be prescribed and therefore relatively certain. Conforming to a statutory duty provides a high degree of protection against claims for breach of confidentiality. In contrast, unregulated professions have to fall back on the broad requirements of the common law of confidentiality and human rights legislation. Publicly funded institutions like universities and colleges will usually have accumulated experience and established procedures based on legal advice to address these circumstances. Private training institutions may be less experienced and are wise to obtain legal advice. One way of introducing a degree of legal clarification is to establish well documented procedures for assessment and any notification of professional bodies, agencies or employers as part of the terms of the training contract with the student that the student accepts on admission and before beginning their training.

Research

One of my difficulties as a researcher is that people are most reluctant to go public about information which really challenges existing practice, the sort of information that could really change things. When ought the good that results from research to override an individual's right to confidentiality?

I had a client who withdrew her permission to publish her story as part of our research only two days before submitting the text for publication. It couldn't have been more inconvenient.

I can't avoid invading people's privacy but I can actively work with their consent by consulting them throughout the research process. Their active co-operation has improved the quality of my research.

Research and confidentiality are contradictory activities. The aim of research is to share new knowledge as widely as possible with others.

The final quotation captures the tensions involved in researching therapy. Such research often involves studying what has been communicated in private, in order to create or discover new knowledge to be communicated to other people, often for the benefit of future clients but which may be disseminated for a variety of reasons. This section is specifically concerned with private information about clients that would normally be protected by confidentiality within therapy. (Medical and social science may involve many other types of information about people, for example derived from observing people in public places or laboratory situations, sometimes involving a degree of deception to protect the validity of the research, but these are not considered here.) Both the British Psychological Society (BPS, 2006) and the British Association for Counselling and Psychotherapy (Bond, 2004) offer guidance on the essential ethical requirements for undertaking research, particularly with regard to consent, trustworthiness and confidentiality. The guidance is based on the relevant law but may suggest ethical requirements where the law is silent or uncertain. Protecting the 'integrity of the research' may create higher standards than those strictly required by law. For example, even when the research is analysed, examined or published in anonymised form, there may be a requirement from the university or a supervisor to see the data before they are anonymised. This should be supported by the subject's explicit consent.

In this section, we are confining ourselves to legal requirements, particularly the general law of confidentiality and data protection. We will distinguish between research which involves studying information where the anonymity of the subjects has been protected; researching personally identifiable information that is not of a private nature; and identifiable information that is personally sensitive or of a private nature.

Anonymous information about subjects of the research

Statistical information and information that that has been thoroughly stripped of personal identification by the therapist would fall into this category. The legal principle that anonymous information is not covered by the law of confidentiality would apply, as developed in the Source Informatics case, provided that:

1 An adequate level of anonymity has been achieved.
2 It is a remote risk that the client might be identified.
3 Care has been taken to exclude the possibility that the client might be identified from the information provided, for example by removing references to any unusual characteristics, descriptions of the client in fine detail, or associations of the client with events described in substantial detail.

Personally identifiable information that is neither private nor personally sensitive

This is an unlikely occurrence in this professional field where the information concerns clients because when someone is identified as having received therapy this will usually be regarded as private information by the courts. However, some research focuses on therapists rather than their clients. Some types of information about therapists may compromise neither the identity of their clients nor the privacy of the therapist. For example, research into the types of client seen by therapists in different settings or analysed according to the therapists' gender does not constitute a significant intrusion on the therapists' privacy and is unlikely to be personally sensitive. Nonetheless, where the person who is the subject of the research is identified or identifiable, the research must be fair (and usually requires prior notice to the subject that information provided by them will be used for research) and have a lawful basis (based on consent, the balance of public interest, or statutory authority).

Some limited exemptions from the usual requirements of data protection may apply, for example where the research is for statistical or historical purposes, if the following conditions are met:

1   The research is conducted in a way that is not likely to cause substantial damage or distress to the person concerned, and
2   The information will not be used to support decisions about particular individuals, and
3   The results of the research are not to be disclosed (in books, articles, reports, dissertations, etc.) in a form that allows identification of the person concerned or for non-research purposes.

Even so, the research subjects should have given their consent to the use of information in research that has been provided for other purposes unless it requires a disproportionate effort to gain consent.

Identifiable information that is personally sensitive or of a private nature

Most case studies and interviews with clients would fall into this category. The definition of personally sensitive information is given in the next chapter but for most practical purposes the content of therapy sessions should be regarded as personally sensitive and therefore subject to strict requirements in terms of consent, protection of the information by adequate security and ensuring that it is anonymised, preferably by someone to whom it was originally disclosed before being passed to a researcher. The law is particularly concerned with preventing the unauthorised disclosure of personally sensitive information and therefore also concerned with protecting privacy and confidentiality. However, this does not fit the needs of all clients or research subjects: some want to be identified in the research in order to have their contribution recognised, to add weight to a social campaign or to challenge assumptions about shame and stigma. The explicit consent of the person concerned is sufficient to permit this. Recording the consent in writing is a sensible precaution against future misunderstanding.

Research ethics emphasise the research subjects' right to withdraw their consent at any point in the research process. What are the legal implications of such a withdrawal? It is not at all clear in law. A withdrawal of consent after publication is probably too late to be effective. The subject may only be able to force a retraction of the research if it is defamatory or for some legal reason other than withdrawal of consent. Results already obtained prior to the withdrawal of consent may be retained by the researcher but further analysis is prevented and the data should either be destroyed or returned to the person concerned. The underlying reasons behind this opinion are based on the idea that processing data, including holding data, requires consent and that once consent is withdrawn those rights cease but only with immediate effect. The distinction between holding data and the results derived from those data fits quantitative research better than most types of qualitative research. In some types of qualitative research, the data are the result, for example extracts from an interview. In these circumstances a withdrawal of consent often requires total exclusion from the study. Securing a well founded consent and actively maintaining that level of commitment throughout the research process is legally and ethically the only way of ensuring the successful completion of the research.

Audit

I worry that some of the audit and management practices in my agency are intrusive on my clients' privacy.

My manager seems to believe that I have committed some form of misconduct. Can I protect myself from investigation by claiming client confidentiality?

Our clients are contracted as seeking the services of our agency rather than to each of us individually so I assume that they are consenting to all the quality checks and controls that we have in place.

It is good management practice for organisations to periodically audit all aspects of their work, including any therapeutic work. Where possible, audits should be undertaken without unnecessarily intruding on personally sensitive information disclosed by clients. This can be assisted by separating financial information and attendance at appointments from any therapeutic notes. Guidance to doctors by the General Medical Council (GMC, 2004) concerning confidentiality asserts that there is an obligation on doctors to participate in audits and that audits should be undertaken in ways that respect patients' confidences by providing information on an anonymous basis wherever possible. If this is not possible and information has to be disclosed in a personally identifiable form, it requires the patient's consent and that the recipients of the personally identifiable information should be bound by confidentiality. Most patients do give their consent when asked. However, there are circumstances when a doctor is required to disclose information regardless of patient consent. For example, the Healthcare Commission, more formally known as the Commission for Health Care Audit and Inspection (CHAI), has the statutory power to require that it is provided with

any information, documents, records (including personal records) or other items

i   which relates or relate to –

  1   the provision of health care by or for an NHS body, or
  2   the discharge of any functions of an NHS body; and

ii   which the CHAI considers it necessary or expedient to have … (Health and Social Care (Community Health and Standards) Act 2003 section 68)

A substantial amount of therapy is provided independent of the health service in other statutory, charitable and commercial organisations. Other statutory bodies may have legal powers to require the production of information and records for audit. Even the sole practitioner working outside an organisational setting is not totally immune to financial audit for taxation purposes, as HM Revenue and Customs has substantial statutory powers to audit taxpayers. However, any organisation has a legitimate interest in reviewing use of resources and the quality of service provided by audit. There is a strong ethical case for arguing that therapists, like doctors, have an ethical duty to participate in audit and to undertake this with the least possible intrusion on clients' privacy. The experience of therapists in the health service is helpful in establishing some basic principles for audit where no statutory powers apply to override the legal requirements of clients' confidentiality and privacy:

- Information for routine audits concerned with finance, resources and level of activity, such as numbers of appointments made and levels of attendance, should be made possible by keeping this type of information separately from any records containing private information about clients, such as records of the contents of therapy sessions.
- All auditors should be bound to confidentiality regarding information about identifiable clients.
- Auditing private information about clients requires justification and checking that the purpose of the audit could not be achieved in some other way. Clients' consent should be sought for audits of their personal records.
- The courts have been willing to override a client's refusal to have their records audited where a greater public interest is at stake, such as the investigation of suspected fraudulent use of resources or serious professional misconduct.
- Intrusion on the therapist's privacy because personally sensitive information about the therapist is included within the client record is probably not sufficient grounds to prevent an audit.

One of the ways this might happen is by the inclusion of personal information about the therapist in any process notes kept within the clients' records. This issue has not been considered by the courts with regard to auditing. However, courts tend to favour protecting the client's interests rather than the professional's where these conflict. Thus, it is legally unwise for a therapist to include any personal information within the client's record that they are not willing to have audited.

What ought clients to be told about professional uses of information about them?

Recent developments in law have moved in the direction of giving clients greater control over what is recorded about them and how that information is used. The law favours the individual being informed about any intrusions on privacy and those intrusions being authorised by that person's consent unless there is some other legal authorisation, such as the balance of public interest or a statutory authority. One of the most practical ways of ensuring that clients are sufficiently informed to give explicit consent is to ensure that the requisite information is included in the client's original contract or service information. An example of such a contract is included in the final chapter. Provided the client is informed about these types of extension of the circle of confidentiality and has not explicitly objected, there is the potential protection for therapists of implied consent when managing unexpected events. Implied consent is a less reliable form of consent because it is inferred from the circumstances rather than a conscious process and therefore more open to challenge than an explicit consent recorded in writing. Nonetheless, implied consent may be both essential and an adequate protection when faced with the unexpected twists and turns of providing therapy. However it is unwise to be over-reliant on implied consent. Implied consent can lead to unexpected misunderstandings. It is always legally preferable to manage issues of privacy and confidentiality by explicit consent, evidenced in writing, whenever possible.

6 Record keeping – Basic Responsibilities

A client was in therapy for PTSD after an accident. The accident triggered other memo-ries and she disclosed a history of severe child abuse which she worked through in the course of her therapy. This was recorded in her notes. When her personal injury case came up in court, the lawyers asked to see the therapy notes. She did not want her fam-ily or the other parties in the case to know about her past. I did not know what to do and I really wished that I had not kept such detailed notes.

I am quite puzzled about what to do about keeping notes. I usually keep brief factual notes with a few reminders of things that I might need for my session with the client. Is this good enough?

I had a client who absolutely refused to allow me to keep notes. I refused to take her on as my agency requires note taking. I am still not sure that that this was fair to the client or what happened to her.

I don't keep notes of sessions as I work in shared premises and can't be sure of ade-quately protecting them when I am not there. I used to take my records to and from home where I could lock them away. Unfortunately, as I was returning home after seeing sev-eral clients, my car was stolen with all the notes locked in the boot. (I was just paying for the petrol.) It was an awful experience telling those clients. I decided that their distress was so much greater than any benefits of keeping records …

Current practice

Current practice by therapists over record keeping is very varied. Some therapists keep extensive notes that combine the information communicated by the client and the therapeutic interpretations of what has been communicated. Some include reflections on their own subjective responses to the client's communica-tions in order to distinguish their client's material from their own and inform their interpretations. This element of therapists' records is sometimes referred to as 'process notes', an essential component of some approaches to therapy. Some ther-apists keep full notes combining process and content which are similar to the full notes that a trainee might be expected to take as the basis for an in-depth case study, or for detailed discussion with a trainer or supervisor. Others keep shorter notes that focus almost exclusively on the content of the client's communications, key events in the session and any therapeutic plans or strategies. Some do not keep any notes at all.

This diversity of practice is the inevitable outcome of different approaches to therapy and different ways in which therapists exercise their professional care for their clients. For some, note taking is an essential activity that provides time for reflection and a useful support to assist in accurately recalling earlier sessions. Others place more emphasis on what the client takes from sessions and brings back with them to the next and therefore are less concerned with maintaining an independent record. Some are concerned that the details in any records held may have the potential to drag the client back to experiences that therapy has helped the client to leave behind, for example if the records were stolen or required in legal proceedings. Therapists walk a tightrope between providing effective care, with all the different interpretations of what this could be, and protecting a client's privacy. The context also matters. Some settings such as clinics place greater emphasis on record keeping than on community support and development. Therapists who work across a range of settings will have experienced the range of expectations and practice regarding record keeping and how these vary according to context, not least the availability of resources to make and store them securely. So it is not surprising that different therapists reach different conclusions about how best to keep records to support their work or may vary their practice for different aspects of their work. Such diversity in practice creates the potential for many different legal concerns about record keeping.

In this chapter we will consider many of the frequently asked questions about record keeping and the law. In order to find the way through this rather complex law, it is useful to distinguish between notification, access and disclosure.

Notification

This is the requirement under the Data Protection Act 1998 to notify the Information Commissioner's Office that personal data are being held. Notification leads to registration of the data holder under the Data Protection Act for the payment of an annual fee. The requirement to notify applies to all computerised records. The *Data Protection Act 1998 Legal Guidance* (Information Commissioner's Office, 2001) provides clarification and is available at www.ico.gov.uk. For further discussion, see below in this chapter.

Access

Access to personal records by the person about whom they are held is governed by the Data Protection Act 1998 and the Freedom of Information Act 2000, together with relevant subsidiary legislation.

All personal data held by public bodies, whether computerised or manual, structured or unstructured, are accessible, subject to certain statutory safeguards, to the person about whom the records are held (the data subject). This includes health, education and social services records, irrespective of when they were made.

Privately held personal records are not subject to the Freedom of Information Act 2000, but they are subject to the data protection legislation (and therefore accessible) if they fall into the category of 'a relevant filing system'. There may also be contractual or equitable rights of access in situations where a statute does not apply. For a discussion of access and its legal implications, see below in this chapter.

Disclosure

By 'disclosure' we mean in this book the sharing of information with another party or organisation, for example, the disclosure of client records to a court, a public authority, or to a relative. The Freedom of Information Act brings personal data which are held by public authorities within the Data Protection Act. Personal data held by all registered data controllers under the Data Protection Act are protected by the legislation from unauthorised disclosure; please see below in this chapter.

Personal data held by therapists outside the Data Protection Act are subject to the therapist/client contract, possibly also to agency practice, and always to professional guidance on best practice within the law relating to confidentiality, discussed further in Chapter 9. We will start with the most basic question about whether there is an obligation to keep records.

Are therapists obliged to keep notes?

There is no legal requirement that all therapists keep records of all their work with clients. Even the professional bodies are cautious about creating such an ethical requirement. The British Psychological Society presents its requirement that psychologists 'should keep appropriate records' as an expression of the ethical principle of respect (BPS, 2006: section 1.2). Although this creates a strong presumption that records ought to be kept, it does not appear to rule out unequivocally that there may be some circumstances where keeping no records is the appropriate action. Not to keep records would require justification. Similarly the British Association for Counselling and Psychotherapy encourages practitioners 'to keep appropriate records of their work with clients unless there are adequate reasons for not keeping records' (BACP, 2007: 5, section 5). Both these ethical statements assume that it is generally desirable to keep records in line with public expectations of professionals. Accurate records provide the basis for accountability. Keeping appropriate records enhances the quality of work undertaken by the therapist by providing an opportunity for reflection when compiling the notes and recording treatment plans; and a point of reference to assist the therapist's recall of significant moments during therapy.

There may be no general legal requirement that notes should be kept in all circumstances but a legal obligation to keep notes can arise in a number of ways. It may be:

- A requirement of the therapist's contract of employment within an agency or organisation.
- A term of a contract agreed with a client who is contributing towards the cost of his or her own therapy.

- A statutory duty imposed on public bodies or agencies within which the therapist is working.
- An obligation to the courts when the therapist is working with witnesses – see the current guidance on working with victims and witnesses. For example, the Crown Prosecution Service (England and Wales) requires that, 'Records of therapy (which includes videos and tapes as well as notes) and other contacts with the witness must be maintained so that they can be produced if required by the court' (CPS, 2005: section 11.4). This requirement concerns the provision of therapy for vulnerable or intimidated adult witnesses. There are comparable stipulations for therapists working with child witnesses (CPS, 2005: sections 3.7–3.14). The Scottish Government has also issued guidance for therapists in Scotland, in the form of its publications "Interviewing Child Witnesses in Scotland" and "Code of Practice to Facilitate the Provision of Therapeutic Support to Child Witnesses in Court Proceedings". Both of these publications are available on the Scottish Government's website at www.scotland.gov.uk.

Recording any breaches of confidentiality is a requirement in some agencies and a wise precaution when working in private practice or as a volunteer. Such a record should include:

- Whether or not the client has consented.
- Any evidence of consent.
- What has been disclosed and to whom, and
- The justification for the disclosure if it has not been authorised by the client affected.

A therapist who is either under a legal obligation to keep records or is ethically committed to doing so may decline to work with a client who refuses to permit the keeping of records.

Some therapists may decide to see clients without keeping any records, if they have the discretion to exercise this choice. The ethical reasons that they may have for doing so might include the deterrent effect of record keeping on some potential clients, for example young people or others who live at the margins of society and mistrust the authorities. In some circumstances, the therapist may have no secure way of protecting records from unauthorised access where they are known to be vulnerable to burglary. In some cases, this may be an exceptional arrangement for a particular client who will accept therapy only on the basis that records are not kept.

The presumption in favour of keeping records means that therapists can expect to be asked by lawyers and courts why they have not kept records. The therapist should make their decision upon the basis of best practice in the prevailing situation, and formally record that decision and the reasons for it. It is wise to have written confirmation that a client has agreed to or required that no records are kept, especially where this is an exceptional arrangement in a service that normally keeps records. In agencies and organisations where not keeping records is routine practice, it is wise to ensure that this practice is included in any agency policy statements or service agreements, and communicated in information to clients and other interested parties in order to avoid misunderstandings. The absence of records will not prevent the therapist being required to give evidence in legal proceedings. On the contrary, anecdotal evidence from therapists indicates that the absence of notes makes it more likely that a therapist will be required to appear in person as a witness for cross-examination. The court has no other way of obtaining the evidence. Where notes exist, it is possible that the submission of those notes or the provision of a comprehensive report based on those notes (which, if possible has been read and approved by the client as accurate), may obviate the need to attend court.

What are the basic legal obligations when records are kept?

Most countries in the European Economic Area (EEA) have already produced legislation or are in the process of producing legislation which regulates almost all aspects of storage, use and disclosure of clients' records by professionals. This creates a shared framework for the management of records across Europe and requires additional safeguards for communications beyond the EEA. This legislation serves two purposes:

1   To protect the privacy of people.
2   To ensure that people about whom information has been collected can check the accuracy of that information.

In this section we will restrict our attention to legal requirements in Europe and in particular to the implications of the Data Protection Act 1998 and Freedom of Information Act 2000. The law is complicated because it is drafted to cover all types of data but we have tried to concentrate on those aspects that are particularly relevant to therapists. Where there are no statutory requirements, legal obligations may arise from common law, a contract of employment and any other legally enforceable contracts.

   One of the reasons for developing this legislative framework was the recognition of the potential power for good and harm posed by computerisation and the ways that this increases the availability of information about people. The legislation is particularly concerned with the regulation of personal data: that is, data which relate to a living individual who can be identified from the data on their own or when combined with other data held by the data controller. If the information is held on a computer, widely defined to include everything from a mainframe to a laptop, there is a duty to notify the Information Commissioner's Office in order to be included in the online register for an annual fee (further details may be obtained from the Office or from the website). Some holders of personal data are exempt but therapists and providers of pastoral care who hold their records on computers are not usually excluded. A reasonably user-friendly nine-step check on whether or not there is a duty to notify can be found on the Information Commissioner's website – see www.dataprotection.gov.uk. Failure to notify when required to do so is an offence punishable by a fine. Notification carries with it an obligation to observe all other requirements concerning data protection.

Personal records that are only held on paper do not require notification. Other aspects of the legislation apply equally to computerised and paper-based records.

The situation with regard to paper-based records is complex, as data protection requirements only apply to manual records that are organised and accessed manually in a 'relevant filing system'. The current diversity of practice in record keeping by therapists means that some are covered by the legislation but others are not. A 'relevant filing system' is defined as 'any set of information' that is structured, either by reference to individuals or by reference to criteria relating to individuals in such a way that specific information relating to a particular individual is readily accessible. In other words, can data about specific individuals be located by a straightforward search? A card index of clients' names organised alphabetically containing their contact details would be a relevant filing system. A client's file that is divided into sections such as name and contact details; reasons for seeking therapy/original referral; information given to client about the therapy and contractual agreements; summary appointments made and sessions attended; correspondence sorted by source; notes of sessions, etc. would constitute a relevant filing system. If the sections are easily identifiable and separated by dividers, someone who is unfamiliar with the contents of the file would have little difficulty in finding upon request correspondence from the client's employer, the reason for the referral, or how regularly the client attends sessions. However, many therapeutic records are not so well organised because information is simply added to the file as it comes to hand, and the file therefore contains a mixture of data stored in chronological order.

Current guidance about what constitutes a 'relevant filing system' specifically excludes records that are simply a chronological record compiled of documents and notes as they come to hand or any other form of haphazard filing. One of the consequences of this is that a client's rights over data held about him or her are better protected by seeing a therapist who makes computerised records or maintains a proper filing system rather than someone who does not keep organised records.

Seeing a therapist who keeps records that fall short of a 'relevant filing system' means that the client *cannot:*

- Require information about the type of data held.
- Ensure that personally sensitive information is held on the basis of explicit consent.
- Be confident of the legal right to obtain a copy of his or her own records.
- Use readily available rights under this legislation as a way of protecting privacy and confidentiality of records, or
- Enlist the support of the Information Commissioner's Office to investigate a potential suspected abuse of the records.

Clients are legally best protected against the abuse of their records if they fall under the terms of the Data Protection legislation. In many ways the burden on the therapist is no greater than that imposed by their professional bodies. There may be some benefits to the therapist in strengthening the legal basis for preventing

Table 6.1   How to identify 'relevant filing systems'

How can I distinguish between 'relevant filing systems' and other types of manual records?

The Data Commissioner recommends applying the 'temp test'. This involves considering whether a temporary administrative assistant (a 'temp') would be able to extract information about an individual without any particular information on the type of work involved or the documents within the files. This test assumes that the temp is reasonably competent and requires only a short induction, explanation and/or operating manual in order for them to access the information. It is not a relevant filing system if the temp requires detailed knowledge of the type of work, the types of records held, or unusual features of records in order to operate it. The Commissioner offers the following example:

John Smith is your employee. He requests details of the leave he has taken in the last six months. You have a collection of personnel files.

(a)   If there is a file entitled 'leave' containing alphabetical dividers the temp would have no difficulty in finding the leave record of John Smith behind the 'S' divider. This is a relevant filing system.

(b)   If there is a file entitled 'John Smith' which is subdivided into categories such as 'contact details', 'sickness', 'pension' and 'leave' the temp would have no difficulty in finding the leave record of John Smith. This is a relevant filing system.

(c)   If there is a file entitled 'John Smith' in a system that only contains the leave record of employees, with leave recorded on standard forms filed in date order within the respective files for each employee, the temp would have no difficulty in finding the record of John Smith's leave taken. This is a relevant filing system.

(d)   If there is a file entitled 'John Smith' but there is no subdivision of its contents, documents are randomly dropped into the file or are filed in chronological order regardless of the subject matter, the temp would have to leaf through the file contents to obtain the information required. This is not a relevant filing system.

(e)   If there is a file entitled 'John Smith' with subdividers that classify the contents of the file in a vague or ambiguous way (such as 'correspondence', 'comments' and 'miscellaneous'), established members of staff only know through experience and knowledge of the particular practice and custom of filing in that system that, for example, leave details are recorded on the back page of a report that is filed in the 'miscellaneous' section. However, the temp would have to leaf through the file contents to obtain the information required because it is not clear from the structure of the file, or from any operating manual, where the relevant information will be held. That would only become clear were the temp provided with additional information specific to that particular workplace and system. This is not a relevant filing system.

For further guidance see: The 'Durant' Case and its impact on the interpretation of the Data Protection Act 1998
http://www.ico.gov.uk/

unauthorised intrusion and providing legal justification for data protection legislation compliant record keeping policies and practice should they be legally challenged or inadequately resourced.

The value to service users in having access to their own notes, particularly in order to correct inaccuracies, was recognised by Parliament when it amended the Freedom of Information Act 2000 to bring all unstructured personal data held by public authorities, particularly health, education and social services, within the scope of the Data Protection Act. This has the effect of requiring that *all* written records, including therapists' records made in these settings, should conform to data protection requirements including the data subjects' right to see a copy of their own records where these have been retained, even if they were compiled many years or decades before the request. Detailed guidance on the specific requirements and exemptions for these agencies can usually be obtained from a specialist within the organisation.

Data protection legislation distinguishes between 'personal data' and 'sensitive personal data' which require higher standards. Most therapists will hold both types of information. Personal data do not have to be about someone's private life but may be information about someone whose identity can be inferred even if the person is not named. It includes any expression of opinion about the individual and any intentions by the record keeper or others towards that person. Personal data might include someone's name, home or work address, income, educational or employment history, provided this information does not imply sensitive personal information, for example that they receive residential psychiatric care, or a religious belief or political affiliation (see below for what is classified as sensitive personal information). The legal basis for holding personal data requires that, before collecting the data, the client should be informed of the identity of the 'data controller'; the purpose for which the data are being collected; and how the data will be used or processed; the client also ought to be informed if the purpose changes after it has been collected (unless this is for the prevention or detection of crime).

The communication of personal data is permitted to protect the vital interests of the data subject. 'Vital interests' do not appear to have been legally defined but the language implies something of substantial interest to the person concerned and therefore excludes trivial matters. A client's consent permits the processing of data that would otherwise be in breach of data protection.

Most of the information held by therapists will be regarded as 'sensitive personal data'. These are data about:

- Racial or ethnic origin
- Political opinions
- Religious beliefs or beliefs of a similar nature
- Trade union membership
- Physical or mental health condition
- Sex life
- Criminality, alleged or proven
- Criminal proceedings, their disposal and sentencing.

The legal right to process sensitive personal information requires greater attention to the data subject's rights. The most significant of these rights is that the recording and use of sensitive personal data require the client's explicit consent. The client has to actively state that they are agreeing to a record being kept and used in the knowledge of the purpose(s) for which the record is being made, how it will be used and any limitations on confidentiality. This should be the routine practice of therapists who hold computerised records or manual records in an organised filing system.

The Data Protection (Processing of Sensitive Personal Data) Order 2000 does permit the keeping of records and their use without explicit consent if it is both in the 'substantial public interest' and for the purpose of discharging 'any function which is designed for the provision of confidential counselling, advice, support or any other services'. We know of no reported cases to guide the interpretation of these requirements. In our view a therapist who relied on these requirements would be required to show that (1) the circumstances prevented obtaining explicit consent or made it inadvisable to do so; (2) a substantial public good was being served; and (3) the sensitive personal data were adequately protected by confidentiality. In such circumstances, it might be reasonable to rely on implied consent or to defer seeking explicit consent until the circumstances permit this. It would not permit recording sensitive personal data against the client's explicit wishes. Communicating sensitive personal data, whether or not they are part of any records, without a client's consent or other legal justification would usually be a breach of the right to privacy under the Human Rights Act 1998 and a common law breach of the client's entitlement to confidentiality. Depending on the circumstances, making an unauthorised disclosure may also create a liability for breach of contract or professional negligence.

The Data Protection Act includes eight principles that guide the legal use of all records of personal data. These require that personal data shall be:

1 Processed fairly and lawfully

Therapists must give clients information as to how they will use information about them. Information should not be obtained by deception and it should be used in accordance with any duties of confidentiality.

2 Obtained only for one or more specified and lawful purposes, and shall not be processed in any manner incompatible with that purpose or those purposes

There is an obligation to inform the client about the purpose for which the data are being recorded. Where a therapist is considering disclosing information to a third party, she must consider how the recipient intends to use the data. If the therapist is aware that the information will be used in any way that is inconsistent with the original purpose, then the disclosure should not take place without the prior informed consent of the client.

3 Adequate, relevant and not excessive
4 Accurate and, where necessary, kept up to date
5 Not be kept longer than necessary

The test for these three principles is what is required in order to achieve a therapeutic purpose? When parts of the notes become irrelevant, are found to be inaccurate, or are no longer required to provide therapy, they should be securely destroyed. Where contact with the client continues over a substantial period of time, these principles encourage a periodical review of the records and 'weeding out' what is no longer required. Chapter 8 provides a case study of how an agency developed its policy to satisfy these principles. Extending the retention of data beyond what is reasonable to provide therapy requires additional explicit consent if sensitive personal data are to be held for those purposes. We return to this issue in the section, 'How long to keep records?' towards the end of this chapter.

The next three principles introduced new rights for the client.

6   The clients' rights must be respected.

The primary function of this principle is to give the clients the right to information about personal data held that relate to them and to a copy of those records. The next section in this chapter provides more detail about these rights.

7   Take appropriate security measures.

This creates a requirement to take appropriate technical and organisational measures against unauthorised or unlawful processing of personal information and against accidental loss or destruction of or damage to notes and records prepared by therapists and other staff. Appropriate safeguards may require:

- Technical security (IT systems).
- Physical security of premises, for instance sensitive information kept in secure locked storage. This includes protecting records from accidental discovery or deliberate interference by others with legitimate access to the premises, such as cleaning or maintenance staff.
- Reasonable precautions against unauthorised access by trespassers and burglars.
- Staff selection and training, for example the training of any secretarial or reception staff in confidentiality. Making confidentiality concerning clients a condition of employment is increasingly common practice in this sector and is consistent with this requirement.

8   Personal data shall not be transferred outside the European Economic Area (All EU Member States plus Iceland, Liechtenstein and Norway).

This may be an issue for clients who move outside the EEA and desire a referral or for therapists whose work requires them to move between the EEA and other countries. A client's consent permits the transfer of personal data.

Clients' right of access to their own notes

The sixth principle of data protection requirement gives the subject of personal data a right to access to the information which is being held about them. This right is referred to as a 'subject access right' to all computerised records and data held in structured manual files. The aim is to enable any citizens to know what information is being processed about them. A written request, proof of identity (if required) and payment of the prescribed fee entitles the data subject to be informed about what data are being processed, for what purpose, to whom it has been or may be disclosed, and to be provided with a copy of those data. This information should be provided within forty days.

Any therapist who is concerned about the client's response to seeing the records may offer to be present and explain the records or to arrange for another suitably qualified person to be present but cannot insist on this. Nor can the release of records be made conditional on the client paying any outstanding fees. The client is entitled to unconditional access.

A client who considers that there is an inaccuracy in the record may ask for it to be corrected with the agreement of the therapist. If there is disagreement about what would be a correct record, it is good practice to include a record of the client's objections in the notes.

If the therapist is concerned that access to the notes would cause serious harm to the physical or mental health of the data subject and that the notes constitute a health record, it may be possible to refuse or defer access with the authorisation of the health professional who is currently or was most recently responsible for the clinical care of the person concerned (Data Protection (Subjects Access Modification) (Health) Order 2000 section 7). The legal presumption in favour of access to personal data makes this an exceptional provision that ought not to be sought or granted lightly.

A client may have rights to see her notes even when there is no statutory right of access to the therapeutic notes because they are 'unstructured' and thus fall outside the requirements of the Data Protection Act. The therapist and client may have agreed access to the notes as part of the contract between them. The client may insist on their production as part of the disclosure of documents for a court case, possibly by the use of a court order. In the last resort, it may simply be unconscionable in the eyes of equity, a longstanding set of legal principles, to withhold access.

Access to notes by others

By other members of the client's family   Adults can insist that a professional protects the confidences contained in records from other members of the family unless the professional is legally required to disclose them, for example as part of the disclosed documents required in family proceedings. Where children or young persons are considered to be sufficiently 'competent' to give their consent to receiving therapy on a confidential basis *and* both the young person concerned and the therapist agree that it is best that the parents are not informed, then the information may be lawfully withheld from someone with parental responsibility (*Gillick v. West Norfolk and West Wisbech Area Health Authority* [1985]). Similarly, information may be withheld from other family members. Possible exceptions to this general principle arise where the disclosure would protect others from serious harm or where a young person's life is at risk.

A young person who is not competent to give consent to therapy cannot be assured of total confidentiality with regard to those with parental responsibility. The therapist ought to take into account the best interests of the young person and the generally positive view that courts take of involving parents unless there are good reasons for not doing so, for example increasing the risk of further abuse. If the therapist is concerned that the child may be subject to abuse, then refer to the government guidance issued under the Children Act 1989 and the Children Act 2004 listed at the end of this book, including *What to do if you are worried that a child is being abused* (DfES, 2006a); *Information Sharing – A Practitioner's Guide* (DfES, 2006b); *Working Together to Safeguard Children: A guide to Inter-Agency Working to Safeguard and Promote the Welfare of Children* (DfES, 2006c); and *Confidentiality: NHS Code of Practice* (DH, 2003a); see also Chapter 4.

After a client's death   In England there is no statutory protection of confidences about someone following their death, nor may a breach of confidence following the death of the confider be actionable (Pattenden, 2003: 639). Despite this lack of legal protection, the normal ethical requirement for health workers and psychological therapists is that respect for confidentiality continues after the death of the person concerned.

Other clients when several clients are being seen at the same time   Information can be disclosed to more than one person at the same time on the basis that it will be treated as confidential by all the recipients. The laws concerning confidentiality would apply.

By journalists and members of the public   The Freedom of Information Act 2000 is a major piece of legislation that requires public bodies and companies functioning as public bodies to respond to requests for information. This legislation has proved invaluable to journalists wanting to discover information held by public bodies, particularly non-personal information such as public policy decisions. Individual citizens can also request information of this type. However, personal information is exempt from this legislation and should be sought under the data protection procedures through the data subject.

By police   The police are not normally permitted access to counselling records. Section 11 of the Police and Criminal Evidence Act (PACE) 1984 specifically treats counselling records as 'excluded material', which gives them additional protection. This protection is not absolute. If the police are investigating a 'serious arrestable offence' they may obtain a warrant from a circuit judge, a more demanding process than the usual search warrants issued by magistrates, which, when granted, will entitle them to access to the client's records.

By lawyers Lawyers have no greater rights of access to therapists' notes than any other citizen. Typically they ask for access to their client's notes on the basis of their client's consent but they may seek a court order that entitles them to access to the notes of their client or possibly to the client notes of another person. Full details about how to respond to a lawyer's request for therapeutic notes can be found in an earlier volume in this series, *Therapists in Court* (Bond & Sandhu, 2005).

By courts Courts of all types carry enormous powers to order the disclosure of therapists' records and may order the therapist to appear as a witness. For a full discussion of the issues see *Therapists in Court* (Bond & Sandhu, 2005).

Who owns the notes?

The question of who owns the notes is usually asked in therapeutic contexts because there is concern over the control of the contents of the notes. The question may arise in organisational contexts because someone more senior in an organisation is seeking access to the contents of the notes. We are aware of this question being asked in health care, education and employee assistance schemes. Behind the question lies an assumption that ownership determines who has control of access to the contents of the notes. This is a mistaken assumption because the law distinguishes between ownership and authorised use of those notes. It is possible to physically own the notes but to be constrained from having access to them or being able to use them because they are held on the trust that they are confidential. For example a company may employ a therapist, pay the therapist's salary and provide the stationery or computing facilities to compile the record. It owns the records. However, it may have required that (and typically will have required that) those records are treated as confidential to the therapist or to the staff who work in that section of the company and the therapist will have worked with clients on this basis. No matter how senior the member of staff, it would usually be a breach of confidentiality for someone outside the 'circle of confidentiality' agreed between the client and therapist to seek access to those notes. Conversely, where there is an agreement that the contents of sessions are made known to or are accessible by other members of an organisation, then the therapist may be required to establish a client's consent to this prior to offering therapy. Both the therapist and agency have a vested interest in striking a balance between deterring clients from accepting a service because client information will be made too freely available and being too restrictive when communicating information. Any changes in practice should be prospective rather than retrospective and will require client consent. Therapists need to ensure consistency between what is agreed with clients and their employer if they are to avoid potential liabilities for either breach of confidentiality or breach of their terms of employment.

In private practice, the notes will belong to the therapist unless there is a contractual agreement to the contrary. If the therapist gives the notes to the client as a client-held record, it is wise to clarify whether the therapist retains ownership or is content for the client to hold both ownership and possession. Ownership of patient-held records in the health service is typically retained by the NHS.

When clients ask about the ownership of notes, they are typically concerned about control over the personal information they contain. In English law, there is no ownership of information, because once it is imparted by one person to another it belongs equally to them both. The clients' best protection lies in their legal rights to privacy and confidentiality. Clients who are paying for their therapy (even if this is only a partial contribution towards the cost) or promising to perform some task in return for receiving therapy can create additional protection for themselves by reaching agreement with the therapist on issues about confidentiality which are more readily enforced as contractual terms. These clients are well placed to create a legally enforceable contract with their therapist in which an agreement about confidentiality and privacy can be clarified and preferably set out in writing.

Process notes

Process notes are an unusual feature of professional practice and unique to some approaches to therapy and similar styles of helping people. They have raised some interesting legal questions over the years but there is no case law from which to give authoritative answers. The perennial questions from therapists are:

'Do I have to give my clients access to my process notes?'

and,

'Am I required to include my process notes if a court requires that I submit all my counselling records concerning a named client?

There is sufficient uncertainty over the answers to each of these questions for a variety of opinions to exist. We will add our opinion by answering each question in turn. In practice, what happens will depend on the circumstances of a specific case. Nonetheless, it is helpful to consider the general legal principles that are likely to be applied.

The distinctive feature about process notes is that they contain information about the subjective processes of the therapist. Some therapists appear to be wary about releasing these notes to legal scrutiny on two accounts. Firstly, these are subjective notes that are being used in a legal culture where objectivity rules and, therefore, are frequently misunderstood and sometimes even ridiculed. Sometimes they are merely tolerated. But this tolerance is often in short supply in an adversarial system of testing the evidence by both sides. The therapist may be making reference to her own life story or subjective processes as a basis for understanding her client better. Sometimes this personal reflection strengthens the empathy for another person's experience. On other occasions, it is used as a way of separating out the therapist's sense of herself from her client's experience so that she can hear another person's experience more clearly. The therapist's sense of herself is a key point of reference in understanding many aspects of the client in most of the psychoanalytic and humanistic approaches to therapy. As a consequence, the process notes are an essential component of some therapeutic approaches but are often more revealing of the therapist than the client. This has led some therapists to ask whether they can withhold them from scrutiny by their client and courts.

When pressed hard, some therapists will argue that they are very uneasy about releasing information gained in the privacy of therapy into a potentially public contest between opposing parties in the courtroom. This unease exists even when the case involves a client and a third party in which the therapist has no direct involvement other than being a witness to the consequences of the event. In such circumstances, it is argued that it is unfair to the therapist and a violation of her privacy to include those parts of records that are primarily about herself. Similarly, therapists are reluctant to give clients access to private personal material that they may have included in their notes but used only indirectly in communications with their client to inform their interventions. Again some therapists argue that this is an invasion of their own privacy and makes them vulnerable to those clients who may be persistently intrusive or predatory.

Our sense from being involved in workshops throughout the UK is that there is a widespread and considerable sense of unease amongst therapists about the disclosure of process notes. It is one of the most contentious issues for therapists about their involvement in any legal processes. What we are about to say is unlikely to ease these concerns.

In our view, if the process notes are contained in the named client's file, or contain named references to a client in another file such as a supervision file, we consider that the client is entitled to copies of these process notes in response to a data subject's access request. A client may also be entitled to records where their identity is not explicitly named but can be inferred. A brief passage from the most thorough recent study of confidentiality indicates the strength of the duty to disclose.

Maintaining dual records – one version for the client and another for the use of the professional – is illegal. Files have to be disclosed no matter how damaging to the professional. Thus the Department of Trade had to disclose records that described the applicant as a 'prat' and an 'out-and-out nutter'. (Pattenden, 2003: 650)

Current trends in the discovery of documents as part of the process of litigation are also against the protection of process notes in order to protect the privacy of the therapist. The law has progressively moved over the last few decades towards a requirement that everything that is discoverable ought to be made available to both sides in all cases. This is believed to provide the best chance of an out of court settlement in civil cases and to increase the likelihood of a fair and decisive hearing should the case be heard in court. It lowers the risk of new evidence being found after the case has been decided. From this perspective, the balance of public interest in ensuring justice outweighs the privacy of both client and therapist. These developments reduce the opportunities for withholding therapeutic documents from court proceedings. However, many documents or parts of documents will not be used if they are not considered relevant to the issues at stake in a particular case. Where there are significant issues of privacy involved for either the client or the therapist, a judge can be asked to review the evidence and decide what is relevant and therefore available for use in the case. A more complete account of the legal issues and process can be found in *Therapists in Court* (Bond & Sandhu, 2005: 19). The therapist may incur legal costs in asking a judge to review documents.

Probably the best way of avoiding or minimising the difficulties posed by process notes is to review one's record keeping practices. Active weeding out of process notes that are not an essential part of the client record and are no longer relevant to the therapeutic process and securely destroying these is a viable option. This destruction must occur before a legal request for disclosure is received. Ideally, it should be part of a record keeping policy and of routine practice. Destroying evidence after a legal request or order is a serious offence. It may also be worth considering whether any of the material included in the process notes goes beyond what is directly relevant to the work with the client and might be better written in a personal journal with no reference to a particular client. It is highly probable that this material would not need to be disclosed to either the client or the courts. The usual test for whether something must be disclosed is based on whether the material is linked to a named client or whether the identity of the client can be inferred. The adoption of these practices reduces the possibility of process notes being problematic but does not totally eliminate the risk for process notes that remain in existence because they continue to serve a therapeutic purpose. The personal journal is not totally immune to discovery. It could be required in cases that directly involve the therapist, such as criminal or civil offences against clients, because of the insights such a journal might offer into the therapist's motives and psychology. However, for ethically conscientious therapists, rethinking the management of process notes is probably the best way to strike a balance between the professional benefits of keeping a record of the subjective therapist's processes while minimising unwanted or damaging disclosures. It is salutary to realise that if a document exists, it is vulnerable to disclosure. There are probably no documents in existence that have total immunity to disclosure in current law.

There is an alternative line of argument in favour of keeping process notes on the same basis as any other notes about a client because they form part of the therapeutic process. If therapists could be confident that these notes would be treated respectfully within the legal process, then this would be much less of an issue. During the preparation of this book we have met a small number of therapists who have either chosen not to weed out this aspect of their records or have been required to disclose records which include process notes that have been treated

respectfully in court. Being able to explain the purpose of the process notes in clear and non-technical language greatly helps in earning the respect of the court.
When writing their records, therapists should constantly ask themselves:

'Can I explain clearly and stand by all that I have written down in my client records and process notes? If I should be asked to explain them in court, could I do so with confidence that they accurately reflect my work with the client and also convey a reasonable standard of therapeutic practice?'

If the answer is negative to either of the questions above, it is the therapist's practice that needs to be changed, not the record.

7 How Long to Keep Records?

I am really unsure how long to keep my records after I stop seeing my client. The books I have advise different times and don't seem to be able to agree with each other.

I stop keeping records as soon as I think that my client won't return. I shred them and dispose of them safely. Is this OK?

My lawyer advised that I should keep my client records for seven years but I know other therapists who are keeping their records for shorter lengths of time based on legal advice and I met someone the other day who keeps hers for ten years. Surely the law can't be so vague?

There is no simple answer to this question. Therapists who seek legal advice may receive very different answers.

The appropriate length of time to keep records depends largely on an assessment of three separate issues:

- An assessment of the purposes to which the records might be put.
- The time limits applicable to different types of legal action and between jurisdictions.
- Time limits for professional complaints and disciplinary procedures.

The law sets time limits for bringing cases in civil law. Time starts running at specified points, e.g. when the cause of action arose, or was first discovered. A legal case may be brought against a therapist, or a client may want access to the notes to provide evidence in a case brought against a third party. It is reasonable to assume that after expiry of the time limits, any records are redundant and can be safely destroyed.

Time limits for bringing legal actions

The law imposes time limits on the bringing of cases before the courts. Since strict general rules might operate unfairly in specific situations, some exceptions have been embodied in statute and developed in case law. For example, in the recent case of *A v Hoare and Others* [2008], the House of Lords has recently considered and revised the law on the discretionary extension of time limits in claims for personal injury based on allegations of past sexual abuse. In a similar way, many professional bodies impose time limits on the bringing of claims and complaints against members. We have considered a number of situations here, but the list is not exhaustive. The law and professional practice in this field is complex, and where consideration is being given to bringing a legal action or making a formal complaint, legal advice or advice from the relevant professional organisation based on the specific circumstances of the case should be sought.

There are few time limits on prosecution for criminal actions, but public interest, the gravity of the offence and the duration of time since its commission, coupled with the nature and weight of the available evidence, may influence the decision whether to pursue prosecution or not. Civil claims in England and Wales are currently regulated by the Limitation Act 1980, as amended. In Scotland they are governed by the Prescription and Limitation (Scotland) Acts 1973 and 1984. In the Law Commission Consultation Paper dated 6 January 1998, the Commission recommended that 'there should be an initial period of limitation of three years that would start from the date the plaintiff discovers, or ought reasonably to discover that he has a legal claim against the defendant… the initial limitation period would be extended where the plaintiff was under a disability, that is, where the plaintiff lacks the capacity to make or communicate decisions, or is under eighteen'. In *Kapadia* v. *London Borough of Lambeth* [2000] CA, the time limit was extended to six years in respect of a person with depression, which the court in those circumstances construed as a disability within the meaning of these recommendations.

In the case of fraud, concealment or mistake, the limitation periods may be postponed: see section 32 of the Limitations Act 1980.

To provide a general idea of the time limits currently operative in law, we have set out here in briefest outline the basic time limits specified for England and Wales by the Limitation Act 1980.

Currently under review, the present time limits are as follows:

12 years

- Specialty Contracts (e.g. under seal) (Limitation Act 1980 s.8).
- Recovery of land (Limitation Act 1980 ss.15 and 17).

6 years

- Tort (other than personal injury or death) (Limitation Act 1980 s.2, but the Latent Damage Act 1986 provides for extension up to a maximum of 15 years if the claimant had no means of knowing that an act or omission might have given rise to the circumstances in respect of which the claim is made).
- Arrears of rent (Limitation Act 1980 s.19).
- Contract (simple) (Limitation Act 1980 s.5).
- Enforcement of judgments (Limitation Act 1980 s.24).

(Continued)

(Continued)

3 Years

- Tort: Personal injury or death (through negligence, nuisance or breach of duty) (Limitation Act 1980 s.11). This many be extended in some cases by the discretion of the court (Limitation Act 1980 s 14 and s 33). See the recent case of *A. v Hoare and Others* [2008] UKHL 6 in which the House of Lords discussed the use of this discretion in cases based on allegations of past sexual abuse.

2 years

- Contribution towards a judgment or arbitration award (Limitation Act 1980 s.10).

1 year

- Defamation (Limitation Act 1980 s.4A).

Table 7.1 shows some of the main types of legal action and their respective limitation periods.

If someone feels aggrieved by the actions of a therapist, they may prefer to make their complaint within a professional conduct or disciplinary procedure. Professional conduct hearings are time-consuming and may create emotional stress but generally involve less financial investment and risk to the complainant than court proceedings. The sanctions that may be imposed in disciplinary proceedings, for example retraining or supervised practice, may be desirable. It is therefore wise to take the time limits for professional complaints into consideration in determining how long to keep records. However, the general trend is away from time limits following *Lewis* v. *Prosthetists and Orthotists* [2001] – which holds that such time limits are not supportable. In this case the only basis for ruling out a complaint that might indirectly arise in relation to the passage of time would be the question of whether it was possible to obtain the relevant evidence.

Time limits for complaints to organisations with responsibility for overseeing professional conduct

We made enquiries of a number of professional organisations to ascertain what, if any, time limits were imposed on complaints against their members. We found that the British Psychological Society (BPS) the United Kingdom Council for Psychotherapy (UKCP), the Health Professions Council (HPC), and the Commission for Social Care Inspection (CSCI) impose no time limits on the making of complaints against their members. However, these organisations recognised that the passage of time may have an impact on the availability and reliability of relevant evidence and therefore may influence the way in which complaints are handled.

Table 7.1   Limitation periods for different types of legal actions

Type of legal action	England and Wales	Scotland
Breach of contract	Complaint to Employment Tribunal for breach of contract of employment: three months from date on which employment ended.	As in England.
	Actions for breach of contract in the civil courts: up to six years from the date on which cause of action accrued. Section 5 Limitation Act 1980.	Up to five years from the date on which the cause of action accrued – Section 6 and Schedule 1 of the Prescription and Limitation (Scotland) Act 1973.
Action in tort for damages for personal injury caused by negligence, nuisance or breach of professional duty of care	Under s. 11 of the Limitation Act 1980, no case may be brought more than three years from the date of the precipitating event, or the 'date of knowledge' of the person injured (i.e. that event caused damage). Actions by children: three years from 18th birthday.	Under the Prescription and Limitation (Scotland) Acts 1973 and 1984, no case may be brought more than three years from the date of the precipitating event, or the date on which the pursuer had knowledge of the relevant facts, or on which, in the opinion of the court, it was reasonably practicable for him to gain that knowledge.
	Time limits for personal injury cases may be judicially extended in some circumstances: see s. 14 (below) and s. 33 of the Limitation Act 1980. See also the recent case of *A v Hoare and Others* [2008] UKHL 6 in which the House of Lords considered the use of this discretion in cases based on allegations of past sexual abuse. In the case of disability, s 28 Limitation Act 1980 allows an extension of time from cessation of disability or death. See also s. 14A Limitation Act 1980 for specific forms of negligence where facts were not known at date of accrual. See also s 14B Limitation Act 1980 for specific forms of negligence not involving personal injury.	Time limits may be judicially extended – Section 19A, 1973 Act.

(Continued)

Table 7.1   (Continued)

Type of legal action	England and Wales	Scotland
Damages in Tort (other than personal injury or death)	Under section 2 Limitation Act 1980, no actions shall be brought after the expiration of six years from the date on which the cause of action occurred, or the 'date of knowledge' i.e. that event caused damage. Actions by children: six years from 18th birthday. No judicial discretion to allow in late cases. For recent examples see *Allen v British Rail Engineering* [2001] and *London Borough of Southwark v Afolabi* [2003]. In case of disability, s 28 Limitation Act 1980 allows the extension of time from cessation of disability or death.	As for personal injury above under the Prescription and Limitation (Scotland) Acts 1973 and 1984. Malcom v Dundee City Council [2007] CSOH 38, Court of Session on 22nd February 2007, is a recent Scottish example, in which the Court refused to exercise discretion to extend time. However, this case did not relate to assault, but was raised under the Protection from Harassment Act 1997.
Applications for compensation for Criminal Injury	Criminal Injuries Compensation Authority (CICA) claims –2 year limitation applies from date of injury.	As in England and Wales.
Criminal cases	No general time limits to bring a prosecution. Some statutes impose limits. Take legal advice regarding specific offences.	As in England and Wales.
Applications to UK courts under the Human Rights Act 1988	One year limit imposed by the Human Rights Act 1998 s.7(5) for bringing proceedings against a public authority.	As in England and Wales.
Actions for libel or slander	One year from the date on which the cause of action occurred. See Section 4A Limitation Act 1980 as amended by s 5 of the Defamation Act 1996. In case of disability, s. 28 (4A) Limitation Act 1980 allows the extension of time from cessation of disability or death.	Three years from the date when the right of action accrued, subject to disregarding any time during which the person alleged to have been defamed was under a legal disability – Section 18A, 1973 Act. Time limits may be judicially extended – Section 19A, 1973 Act.

The British Association for Counselling and Psychotherapy has a policy relating to complaints against members which is set out in the Ethical Framework (BACP, 2007), within which complaints against members can be lodged either:

a) within a reasonable time of the alleged professional misconduct; *or*
b) within three years of the ending of the professional relationship; *or*
c) within three years of the date when the Complainant reasonably became aware of the alleged professional misconduct.

The complainant must provide a written explanation as to when/how they became aware and this will be considered by the Pre-Hearing Assessment Panel which will decide if the explanation given is good and/or sufficient.

The General Medical Council operates a five-year limit on all complaints unless the Registrar considers that it would be in the public interest to investigate: see 'The General Medical Council (Fitness to Practise) Rules Order of Council 2004' at para 4 (5):

No allegation shall proceed further if, at the time it is first made or first comes to the attention of the General Council, more than five years have elapsed since the most recent events giving rise to the allegation, unless the Registrar considers that it is in the public interest, in the exceptional circumstances of the case, for it to proceed.

For further details see the GMC website at http://www.opsi.gov.uk/si/si2004/20042608.htm. The impact of the general consensus amongst organisations overseeing professional conduct to impose no time limit on the making of complaints is that, if a therapist is looking to self-protection, he may be inclined to retain records indefinitely. This is in contrast to the provisions of the Data Protection Act 1998 which provides that sensitive personal data should be kept only as long as is necessary. We are not aware of any court cases on this issue. Since the Human Rights Act 1998 applies equally to therapists and to clients, when forming a policy about keeping records it seems both legally and morally just that the needs and rights of both should be respected and protected.

Policy and practice in record keeping

Consideration of legal implications requires attending to the balance between private and public interests. Personal values and philosophy also need to be taken into account. In an area of such complexity, and one where it is impossible to anticipate all eventualities, there is always the possibility of a cause of action emerging long after the event, a case going wrong, or being challenged over exceptional issues that do not fit a practitioner's or agency's values. These will usually be rare events, but cannot be totally avoided by busy therapists. One way of preparing for being challenged on the exceptional case and testing your values related to record keeping is to ask yourself:

> 'When I am challenged on my policy and practice over record keeping, which would I prefer to be known for – being over-zealous in attending to my clients' rights or attending to my own need to be self-protective? In a situation where I may be damned for whatever I do, which I would prefer to stand for? Where do I consider the balance between the private and public interests to lie?'

Lawyers experienced in defending professionals against negligence and other civil claims will usually advise keeping records for as long as necessary to ensure that time has expired for these types of action. Insurers who provide cover for professional liability may prefer records to be as full as possible and kept for as long as possible to provide the best possible protection for therapists in case they are sued or subject to professional disciplinary proceedings. These opinions are directed at providing the professional with the maximum protection. On the other hand, lawyers grounded in human rights or data protection are more likely to prioritise the clients' interests, especially their privacy, and therefore minimise the length of time for which records ought to be kept.

Therapists have to find a balance between differing legal views in order to develop a position that is appropriate to the circumstances of their work. The data protection requirements are an attempt to reconcile these opposing tensions.

One way forward where there may be a foreseeable tension between the client's, the therapist's and any agency's interests in how long records are kept, is to discuss these issues with the client and to agree upon appropriate action. The therapist or their employing organisation may have a firm policy which the client may choose to accept or reject. Chapter 8 describes how a counselling service developed its policy on this issue.

8 Record Keeping – A Case Study*

Data protection legislation has changed the way professionals keep records. Those who write records should respect the people concerned and write bearing in mind that the records might be read by the person concerned or others with legal access to them.

This chapter considers the challenges of meeting the Data Protection Principles set out in schedule 1 of the Data Protection Act (DPA) 1998, in particular:

'Personal data shall be adequate, relevant and not excessive in relation to the purpose or purposes for which they are processed.' (Schedule 1 paragraph 3)

'Personal data shall be accurate and, where necessary, kept up to date.' (Schedule 1 paragraph 4) and

'Personal data processed for any purpose or purposes shall not be kept for longer than is necessary for that purpose or those purposes.' (Schedule 1 paragraph 5)

This case study also demonstrates how poor record keeping can create legal liabilities for the people concerned as well as undermine the therapeutic usefulness of records.

The events recorded in this case study are fictitious but are not untypical of issues faced by counsellors in similar circumstances. A case history is provided. It is written as a reasonably full account of the counsellor's observations, feelings and reflections. These observations are too unsystematic for case notes so the therapist is required to select the important features to be included in her record of her work. The records created by the counsellor are provided with some questions to consider. Some answers and suggestions can be found in the commentary that follows the case study.

---

*This chapter has been contributed by Kirstie Adamson, drawing on her experience as a lawyer specialising in family law before commencing work full time as a counsellor, including school counselling.

CASE STUDY JOHN

Case History Session 1

John appeared in the counselling room in tears. He was a small boy with blond hair falling into his eyes, slight of build with a wary and cautious look.

He hurriedly asked if he could come and talk. It was break time and unusually I happened to have a space the next session so I said that would be fine and ushered him in, closing the door. He came in, more hesitant now that he knew he could come, and sat down on the edge of his seat sniffing occasionally and looking down.

I asked him gently what had happened. He looked up, and then looking down again began to talk. He had been in a group of people and some of them had started name-calling someone in the year below. He hadn't liked it but had not known what to do. He had said one thing. That was all – not half as much as the others. But everyone had reacted when he had spoken and had pushed them together as if to fight. Before the group knew what was happening, a tutor had waded in and demanded to know what was going on. Now John had heard that the younger boy had said that it was him who had been the ringleader. John's voice rose at this point and became more urgent, entreating almost. I found I wanted to believe him.

He told me that he was often wrongly blamed for other things just because he was present. What worried him the most was that he had already had one warning and did not want another. He talked about how angry he felt when he was blamed without his story being heard. He wanted to go and hurt someone, something – and had punched a wall.

We looked at what was possible for him now. He was clear that no one was going to own up and if the younger boy said it was only him then that is what people would believe. He was worried that they would say that he had hurt the boy, but he hadn't. I suggested he wrote down his version of what had happened and talked to his tutor. He was happy about that and went away calmer. We agreed a further session next week.

Counselling record for Session 1

13-year-old boy. Involved in a fight with a younger boy whom he pushed. Concerns about anger and bullying and being blamed for things he has not done. This is not the first time.

Agreed that he would write down his version of events and speak to his tutor about it.

Questions

1   How accurate is this account?
2   How might this record create legal liability for the client, the counsellor or the institution?

Case History Session 2

Next week John came in looking pleased to be here. I felt like I was providing a refuge to this boy. He had told his parents all about last week's incident and they had been very angry that he was being blamed for something he didn't do. They had been up at the school, shouting at the head. John said that the head teacher had insisted that the boy concerned and John sat down together and talked about the incident. John proudly told me that he was helping the other boy and making sure he was OK.

Counselling record for Session 2

Explored John's feelings about last week's incident. Feeling supported by parents. Pleased that they were angry on his behalf. He had found it very difficult to talk with the victim but was enjoying helping him now.

Question

What has been distorted in this record?

Case History Session 3

The next session John did not come. I sent a note to his class asking him to come to reception. He came to see me the following day looking very worried and almost scared. He was reluctant to talk at first but when I pressed him he acknowledged that he hadn't forgotten. I asked him what had stopped him coming. Eventually he said that his parents had seen the note that I had sent to the class and had forbidden him to come to counselling again. As he said this he looked very scared. I wanted to know what John himself wanted. So I asked him what he wanted to do. He said he wanted to come but he was scared. I reassured him that he could make a decision about whether he wanted to come or not and that it was nothing to do with his parents. They could not refuse to allow him to come. He started to relax. I asked him more about his parents. I wanted to know more about what sort of people they were. I felt outraged. How dare they just forbid him to come! Things were clearly difficult for him and if counselling was helping, what right did they have to stop him?

I suggested we look at his family with shells and stones. He chose a great big rough stone for his father, a mussel shell for his mother, a neatly curved shell for his elder sister and a small stone for him. He placed his mother next door to his father, his sister the other side of his father about an inch away and then he placed himself about three inches away from anyone, about equidistant between his mother and his sister. He was very reluctant to talk about why he had chosen the shells and stones and what they might signify. So I asked him would he like to change any of the positions if he could? He said that he would like to be closer to his mother and sister but that was not possible. I asked him what might be possible. He thought hard and said it might be possible sometimes for him to be closer to one or the other but not both at the same time. I asked him again whether he wanted to move any of the other shells or stones. He looked again and said that he wanted his father's stone to move far away, far enough so that he could not touch him. I asked him what he meant and he clammed up and would not say any more.

(Continued)

(Continued)

I was curious now and was sure that there might be very difficult family dynamics. I felt pleased that I had persuaded him to continue with counselling.

As he left, a member of staff was coming round the corner to see me. She saw him and when he had passed out of sight she said, 'Oh not him'. I said, 'He's been through a hard time' and felt even more convinced that he was somehow being maligned and was not being given a fair hearing. She raised her eyebrows. 'And you believe him?' I said 'Yes. Are you saying you don't?'

'He's very good at talking but only the other week he was seen thumping a younger boy but he is still denying it.'

'He told me he only called him names and pushed him once.'

The teacher responded, 'He'll say anything', and went away shaking her head.

I was now late leaving work and packed up in a hurry, forgetting that John's notes were lying on the table. I only remembered that I had not put everything away when I reached home. I had been distracted by thinking about what the teacher had said. Fortunately I was in early on the next day but found that the door was unlocked so anyone could have come in and read his notes. I was relieved when they didn't look as if they had been disturbed in any way. If I hadn't been coming in early, I would have phoned to ask someone in reception to use the key that is kept there to return the notes to my filing cabinet.

Counselling record for Session 3

Parents told him not to come to counselling but he still wants to come. Looking at family dynamics with shells and stones. Some difficulties within his relationship with his father.

Questions

1 What issues about consent and confidentiality are raised by this session, that require the counsellor's attention?
2 What significant information is omitted from the notes?

Case History Session 4

The following week John did come for his session. I was just beginning to wonder whether he was coming when he came in looking rather hangdog. I asked him what was wrong. He said he had a headache.

He looked downwards, fiddling with the straps on his bag as if not sure what to say next or what he wanted. I was just about to ask him a question about last session when he launched in talking about his friends. He did not have many friends. He found it difficult to talk to people. They did not seem to understand him. I kept thinking about how we had left the last session and wanted to know what he had been getting at.

I asked him who he did talk to, who listened to him. He hesitated for a long while and then looked up relieved. 'My dog, of course.' He smiled, with his face going gentle at the thought of her. I invited him to say more about his dog. He talked about how she listened to him and he could say anything to her.

'So what about people, who would you talk to?'

'I don't need to talk.' His face started closing down again.

'So what about your parents?' I pressed on.

'I don't want to talk to them, I'd just get shouted at' – his voice suddenly went quieter – 'or hit.'

I needed to be sure I had heard what I thought I had. 'I didn't quite catch what you said at the end there.' He was quiet for a bit and then blurted out, 'Sometimes my dad hits me if I go on too much.'

'So what actually happens?'

'Well last night he pushed my head against the wall, cos I argued about what we watched on telly. It hurts now at the back of my head.'

'Has this happened before?'

'Yes he's hit me on the arms with rulers. It's been like it for ages. Sometimes I have red marks, there's a scratch which he made last time, it had a sharp bit on which caught me' – pulling up his sleeve and showing me a scratch on his forearm.

'Has he hurt you before like last night?'

'He's given me bruises when he grabs me and shakes me.'

'How often does this happen?'

'About two or three times a week but mostly he doesn't leave marks.'

'Who else knows about this?'

'No one, you're not going to tell anyone, are you? I'll get into worse trouble.'

'I do think that someone needs to be told. It's not OK for you to be hurt.'

'Please, look, it's feeling better now. If anything else happens then you can tell some-one then or I will, but not this time. Please.'

I sighed and agreed that I would not tell anyone.

Counselling record for Session 4

Isolated, hard to talk to anyone. Arguments with family especially father who on occasion hits him with ruler and leaves marks. Incident last night – when J's head was pushed against the wall and is still hurting today.

Questions

1   What is missing from this record?
2   What issues are raised by these disclosures and John's request for silence?
3   Does the counsellor have any duties or responsibilities in regard to child protection in respect of this child?

Case History Session 5

Next session John came in quite jauntily. He sat down and started to talk about friends or the lack of them. But he seemed quite buoyant, very different from the child I had seen last week. I suggested we use a game about self-esteem. As he moved nearer to the board he knocked his arm against his chair and winced. I asked him what he had done and he said he had been playing rugby. Another kid had stamped on him in a scrum and it was painful. I asked him when this had happened and he said it was earlier that day. I believed him and we went on with the session.

Counselling record for Session 5

Issues around friends and self-esteem. Looking at self-esteem issues through play-ing the esteem card game.

Question

What is missing from the records?

Events between sessions ...

The next day I got a message that the deputy head wanted to see me. She was clearly worried, saying that John had told the PE teacher that his arm had been hurt by his father and that the counsellor knew about it. She said that they were very worried about him and was concerned as to why I had not informed anyone. I explained what John had said to me. I was told that he had not had rugby in school that week. She asked me to write a full report about the session and anything else relevant that had come up in the sessions. I did this and handed it to the deputy head. She read it quickly and when she reached the part about the previous sessions her expression became very serious.

'This is worse than I thought it was. We are informing social services. It's not the first time that he has talked about being hurt by his father. They may want to talk to you.'

'That's fine. I'll be happy to talk to them.'

Left thinking that I ought to discuss this case in supervision.

No notes

Questions

1   Should there have been a note in the counselling record of this conversation?
2   What would be an adequate record of this discussion?
3   What issues are raised by the deputy head's request for information from the counsellor?

Case History Session 6

The following week John came into the session and sat down saying he did not know what to talk about. I asked him about the last session, saying that he had said that he had hurt his arm playing rugby but that I had since discovered that his father had hurt him and wondered what had stopped him being able to tell the truth here. He looked down silently and then gradually began to speak slowly. He was not sure why he had not been able to talk about it but he was also not sure that I would do anything about it. He talked about having to meet with a social worker, whom he did not like. He said no one was talking to him at home. I acknowledged that social services had contacted me and asked me to write them a report about our sessions. He shrugged his shoulders.

I had received a letter from social services stating that they were holding a child protection investigation in respect of John and requesting a report from me about my work with John. I summarised our sessions and the information regarding his family that John had told me and said that I was unable to come to the meeting.

Counselling record for Session 6

Exploring briefly the story he told in the previous session about his injury. Feeling isolated within family. Difficulties with his relationship with social worker.

Questions:

1   What would be a more adequate record of these events?
2   Where can the counsellor find guidance on consent, disclosure and writing a report about her work with John in response to the request from social services?
3   Who can make decisions about John's therapy?
4   In what circumstances can social services make decisions for a child about their therapy?
5   What issues are raised by the use of the records for the counsellor's research and extending the period for which they are kept?

Missed session

The following week he was not present for our session. A few days later I received a letter from social services relating to the decisions made at the conference saying that John had said that he no longer wanted to see the school counsellor.

I felt that we had gone through a lot in our sessions, and as I was just about to start some research about counselling in schools I decided that I would keep John's records longer than the fixed period that I had agreed with the school. They might prove useful in my research.

No notes.

Commentary on the record keeping

From a legal perspective, these notes are relevant and certainly not excessive. On the contrary, they are frequently inadequate and sometimes inaccurate in ways that could create problems for the people concerned. Greater awareness of the potential legal issues involved in a case of this sort would have helped the counsellor produce records that provided better protection of her client's interests and supported the therapy better. Improved record keeping would help the counsellor to identify and reflect on her responsibilities in this case and the associated legal issues that go beyond record keeping. These records would leave both the counsellor and the school poorly placed to fulfil their obligations to pupils and vulnerable to potential litigation. Although there is currently no professionally endorsed method for writing records, and styles may vary, legal analysis helps to identify some of the issues that ought to be considered when making therapeutic records.

Session 1 Anyone reading these notes would be misled into believing that John had admitted to pushing the younger boy, whereas John stated that they were 'pushed together'. This is a potentially serious inaccuracy.

If the boy had suffered a head injury from being pushed then it is possible that this incident could be looked on as a criminal assault. The seriousness of the offence would depend on the seriousness of the injury. If the Crown Prosecution Service found out that John had been having counselling then they would probably ask for disclosure of his counselling notes. They would be looking for confirmation and details of the assault. As written, these notes appear to confirm that John was responsible for an assault. The more serious the crime, the more serious the potential impact on John of inaccurate notes. John's age will also be a significant factor in the consequences for him. If under ten he is under the age of criminal responsibility, but if he is exhibiting extreme aggressive behaviour he may be 'a child in need', or a child suffering (or at risk of suffering) significant harm, and therefore might fall within the child protection provisions.

The records could also become significant evidence in other types of legal case. If the victim had suffered a head injury with a lasting effect, he might want to make a claim to the Criminal Injuries Compensation Authority. He would need to prove that the incident had happened as a result of a crime of violence committed by John and that he was an innocent victim. Alternatively, the victim could claim for negligence against the school if he could prove that John was of known violent character and the school had knowingly placed him in a position where he was likely to be attacked by John. To support his claim, the boy's lawyers might seek third party disclosure of John's counselling notes. In England and Wales, section 31(12) of the Civil Procedure Rules governs the right to apply for disclosure. A judge would have to be convinced that these documents were relevant and that their importance was such that it justified their disclosure. A similar disclosure of records could be sought in Scotland by way of a procedure known as 'commission and diligence'.

It is possible for a claim of negligence to be made against the therapist where it can be demonstrated that their actions, e.g. making inaccurate records, resulted in someone suffering a loss.

Session 2   Does the report of John's emotions fit what was said to the counsellor? A single example failing to adequately capture a client's feelings that are marginal to the course of events is unlikely to carry legal significance but might be therapeutically significant. The therapist may be missing John's conflicting emotions and ambivalence. When errors of this type accumulate, they are more likely to become apparent to others and the counsellor's competence may be questioned.

Session 3   This is a therapeutically significant session arising from complex events and requiring the counsellor's use of her judgement in how best to respond to the issues raised. On any assessment, these notes are inadequate. Better notes would have referred to the non-attendance of the planned session; John's report of his parents' reaction to discovering the counsellor's note; the counsellor's reasons for overriding the parents' refusal to permit counselling; and a more adequate record of the work undertaken with the shells. The positive relationships with his sister and mother are completely omitted.

There are other significant omissions to the records that may be due to a lack of relevant legal knowledge. Someone with parental responsibility, who may or not be a biological parent (see Chapter 11), can refuse permission for children to come to counselling. The refusal will be ineffective for children over 16 as they are considered sufficiently competent in family law to make decisions on their own behalf. The situation is more complex for children under 16. In order to override a refusal by someone with parental responsibility, the counsellor should have conducted an assessment to determine whether the young client is capable of making a decision on his own behalf (*Gillick* v. *West Norfolk & Wisbech Area Health Authority* [1985]). Children and young people are considered competent to make decisions on their own behalf when they are able to fully understand the situation and can come to an informed decision, having considered all the implications. This has come to be known colloquially as 'Gillick competence' (see Chapter 11). The notes should record that this assessment has taken place and should note the questions and answers and any other significant information on which a decision about the child's competence was reached.

In cases where a child who is suffering or at risk of suffering significant harm has been subject to child protection proceedings, the Family Court can make a variety of protective orders in the best interests of the child. Under some of these court orders, the court can direct a medical or psychiatric examination or assessment of a child. Where there is a care order in force, the local authority shares parental responsibility with the child's parents or carers, and, where necessary, can override their decisions, for example about therapy. Usually, this would involve consultation with the parents and seeking their positive involvement.

Exceptions to parental involvement may arise when a child or young person is considered sufficiently competent to insist on confidentiality or it is considered that involving the parents would increase the risk to the child, for example if the parent is suspected of abusing the child. If the professional is involved in assessments and any consultations with other professionals in order to inform decision-making within the child protection process, details should be included in their notes.

There is a defined system for collecting and sharing child protection information within schools and referral on to social services which is described in *Working Together to Safeguard Children: A guide to inter-agency working to safeguard and promote the welfare of children* (DfES, 2006c). This requires that a person is nominated in each school to be responsible for child protection liaison. The procedures are set up by the Local Safeguarding Children Boards (formerly the Area Child Protection Committees) for each county and set out in the Local Education Authority's child protection guidelines for schools. Copies should be available in all schools. The references at the end of this book contain additional resources on child protection law, practice and procedure in England and Scotland.

Confidentiality can be more difficult within a school where the free exchange of information between staff is routine practice.

Confidentiality curtails what a counsellor can communicate. It excludes casually discussing clients with a fellow teacher, however much the counsellor might want to stick up for her client. Where it is helpful for teachers to know the counsellor's concerns, this should normally only be done with the consent of the child unless it is a child protection issue being reported to the member of staff identified as responsible for this area of work. The records show no evidence that John has been either informed about any limitations to confidentiality (see later) or that he has given his consent to discussion with the teacher. There is also the issue of whether John is of sufficient age and understanding and has a good enough grasp of the circumstances to be considered 'Gillick competent' to give his consent on this issue or not (see Chapter 11).

In extreme cases if a counsellor does disclose confidential information unnecessarily about counselling sessions and this causes loss or damage to the child, then the counsellor can be sued for damages or other remedies. Complaints can also be made to the school, Local Education Authority or the counsellor's professional body.

Leaving records out where they can be seen by others is negligent. If these records had got into the hands of anyone else then the counsellor or the school could be sued for negligence. All confidential records need to be stored in a secure safe place at all times, i.e. in a locked cabinet with appropriate security measures in place.

Leaving a key to the filing cabinet that is freely available to all staff, particularly those outside the circle of confidentiality, breaches the data protection requirement to keep records securely.

Session 4 Again the notes are inadequate. John's late arrival is therapeutically significant because of what the lateness may indicate about his motivation towards counselling or practical difficulties he may be encountering. The significance of the dog is also omitted. This is the second omission of positive attachments that are significant in understanding this boy's circumstances. Noting both positive and problematic relationships is all the more important when working with young people whose parental relationships are unstable or abusive. Positive relationships are not only useful resources in therapy but may become significant information in the event of any interventions by other professionals to protect the child from further abuse, which is starting to look a possibility by the end of this session.

Recent developments following the Children Act 2004 have reinforced the child protection provisions of the Children Act 1989. Professionals working with children have a responsibility to ensure that they are aware of their responsibilities for safeguarding and promoting the welfare of children. This may involve sharing information between professionals, agencies and Local Safeguarding Children Boards. For relevant guidance, see DfES, 2006b, 2006c, and Scottish Executive, 1998, 2003a, 2003b, 2003c, 2004a, 2004b, 2006).

In this session, the counsellor is told directly for the first time of actual physical harm to John inflicted in the home. The lack of adequate notes creates potential legal liabilities. If John was more seriously injured than at first appeared, the counsellor's role as employee of the school carries additional legal implications: for example, the school would be deemed to know about the injury whether or not the counsellor had informed others in the school. Thus, the school could potentially be sued for not acting soon enough to protect him. If the counsellor was sufficiently concerned, she should have liaised with the school child protection officer to consider what to do next. A school is required under local child protection procedures to report to social services situations where child abuse is suspected.

If the counsellor were self-employed then the school could defend itself by stating that they had not been informed. The information was held by the counsellor and therefore the counsellor is responsible and legally liable for actions taken (or not taken). Regardless of how the counsellor was employed, she would have been wise to record what the client reported about the cause of the injury, her own direct observations of the injury and any actions taken. If no action is taken, it is good practice to state the reasons for this. Self-employed counsellors working with children and vulnerable adults should make themselves aware of the local procedures for protection and referral, and ensure that they know how they should be implemented. Advice and guidance are usually readily available from the relevant local authority and are also often supported by publicly available policies and procedures on the web. Recent developments in policy and practice to protect vulnerable children are readily available as non-statutory guidance from www.everychildmatters.gov.uk. This includes guidance on *What to do if you are worried that a child is being abused* (DfES, 2006a) and *Information Sharing – A*

Practitioner's Guide (DfES, 2006b). The outline practice and procedure of inter-agency co-operation in child protection is set out in *Working Together to Safeguard Children: A guide to Inter-Agency Working to Safeguard and Promote the Welfare of Children*, (DfES, 2006c), the first eight chapters of which are issued as statutory guidance, mandatory in England under s. 7 of the Local Authority Social Services Act 1970. This means that the Guidance must be followed, and any departure from it must be justified in any subsequent complaints procedure or judicial review. The remaining chapters are non-statutory practice guidance. This publication sets out clearly the levels of co-operation expected from social services, schools, health professionals, police and others, and the inter-agency procedures for child protection. Schools have further specific duties under the Education Act 2002. For Scotland, see the Education (Scotland) Act 1980 and the Education (Support for Learning) (Scotland) Act 2004.

Session 5   Further evidence of injury is revealed by the client but this is not reported, nor is his explanation included in the rather scanty notes.

Between sessions: Events between sessions that relate to the client ought to be recorded. The different version of events provided by the deputy head, the request for the report and a copy of the report ought to be included in the notes. Similarly, discussion about clients in supervision ought to be summarised in the notes. It is not clear in this case whether such discussions took place.

Session 6   Communications from other agencies about the client ought to be referred to in the notes and a copy of any written or electronic communication ought to be included in the file. The notes appear to lay all responsibility for any difficulties in the referral to social services on a poor relationship with a social worker, which arguably has been weakened by the counsellor's poor management of the client's expectations over confidentiality.

Missed session   Missed sessions should be noted.

Using the records for research   The DPA requires that records should not be kept longer than necessary for the purpose(s) for which they were compiled, and a retention of records containing sensitive personal data must be authorised by explicit consent. The counsellor's proposal to keep counselling records without additional consent from the subject of those records breaches this requirement. Any consent that extends or limits the use of the records should be noted in the records.

What would be adequate records?

The inadequacy of the notes in this case study is compounded by the lack of any attempt to establish the client's understanding of the level of confidentiality that he was being offered. Establishing an adequate understanding over confidentiality would have been more ethically respectful of the client and would also have established the counselling on a sounder basis. In addition, it would have provided a point of reference from which the counsellor could have avoided many of the ethical and legal difficulties that arose. Issues of consent are considered more fully in Chapter 9. Recording the nature of the confidentiality offered to clients and any agreed limitations should be included within the case file.

Even though this is a fairly typical case for a school counsellor, the commentary indicates how commonplace issues that occur when providing therapy can touch on many different aspects of law. This raises the question 'What would be an adequate set of records for the work with this client?' The examples provided in the case study indicate how *not* to write case notes or records. In particular, there were significant factual errors in the records of the first session with this client. Such notes would not meet the data protection requirements that a record should be should be 'adequate, relevant and not excessive' and 'accurate'. A much better set of notes for the first session would have been:

John   **aged 13**   **Date of session**

Drop in session. Client was present while others called a younger pupil names. When client also said something he was pushed into the younger pupil. Tutor arrived and client was blamed by younger pupil. Client upset that he is being wrongly blamed. Client – angry that he has not been listened to and fears that he won't be believed in any event. Hurt himself in anger.

Agreed that he would write down his version of events and speak to tutor. Agreed session for next week.

---

9 Sharing Information between Professionals

If I write down everything that she tells me at school, will I have to disclose it all if there is a child protection investigation later on?

The police just came to the office one morning and asked to see my notes ...

I asked the doctor if he could help P next time he saw her with advice about her diet – he asked why, but I was not sure if I was at liberty to tell him ... so I just said 'look, trust me on this one ... '(GP surgery counsellor)

I had worked with the parents in couple therapy. They decided to divorce, and they went to mediation for money issues. They could not agree and then he called me, wanting me to write and tell the mediator what she had said in therapy about her gambling, because now she is refusing to admit that it is a problem ...

The working environment for therapists is changing rapidly. Recent developments in management theory and government policy have placed greater emphasis on the benefits of multi-agency working and collaboration within multi-professional teams. The creation of electronic records has opened up new possibilities for record sharing within and between services, for example health, social care and child protection. The increasing emphasis on preventative work in services for children and adults, especially those who are considered vulnerable to neglect or abuse, requires the sharing of information more freely and at an earlier stage than has been customary in the past.

As Pattenden (2003: 13) points out, a duty of confidentiality may be created when a professional acquires confidential personal information. The Human Rights Act 1998 (HRA) provides the background for enforcement of individual rights, the Data Protection Act 1998 (DPA) applies to the collection, processing and storing of personal identifiable information, and the Freedom of Information Act 2000 (FOIA) includes additional law that applies the DPA principles to records held by public bodies. Our problem is that we have to respond appropriately in the context of this complex legal framework and within the specific political, contractual, policy and practical demands of our work environment.

Therapists who work within public and private service and agency settings are increasingly facing expectations that they will change the way they work in order to fit into new organisational structures and practices. The law is a relatively loose framework that is possibly more open to change than professional custom and practice. In this chapter we will not consider the overall benefits or losses of professional practice developments, but we will look at the legal issues that arise from these changes, considered in the context of specific situations.

In the context of the current political trend towards policies embodying greater openness, transparency and information sharing, it seems likely that, in future, some therapists will be requested, or even required, to keep their records in a shared paper based or electronic filing system. For many therapists, this will raise questions of policy and of practice – 'How can I be sure that this is a legally valid requirement?' and 'Can I resist such a demand?' and 'On what grounds would resistance be justified?' These questions involve the interaction of a complex mix of law and practice issues and we regret that there are no hard and fast answers. At the end of the day, therapists will have to make their own decision, but to assist, below is a summary of the current law and practice guidance relevant to these questions. Bear in mind that this is a fast developing area and watch out for changes in law and practice; the websites listed at the end of the chapter may prove helpful.

What are the legal issues involved in keeping records in a shared filing system?

Within the health professions, there is a fundamental presumption of patient/client confidentiality, but in the current trend towards team and inter-agency working, particularly in the fields of health and social services, the circle of people with access to confidential information is widening. GP practices may comprise practitioners, nurses, administrative and managerial staff and others providing various therapeutic services, some or all sharing access to computer-based and/or written patient records. Despite the recognition by the British Medical Association (BMA) and the General Medical Council (GMC) that patients have a right to expect that information about them will be held in confidence by their doctors, this is interpreted to include everyone in the 'health care team' involved, for example all the members of a GP practice. All these, and temporary staff, may have access to client data through a shared system. Protection of client confidence requires the regulation of unauthorised access to sensitive data and comprehensive data handling procedures to protect client information – anti-burglar precautions for offices, passwords and firewalls for computer systems, etc. (Pattenden, 2003: 428–431).

In addition, there are increasingly complex infrastructures, including the evaluation and audit of health and social services, and interestingly, the GMC guidelines (requiring express consent for the disclosure of confidential patient-identifiable information for research, education, administration or audit) are stricter than those of the NHS, in which implied consent is acceptable (Pattenden, 2003: 430–431).

The impact of all this is that in health and social care, clients cannot expect that the information they give to their doctor or social worker stays with that person individually. They should expect, however, that they will be given information in broad terms about the boundaries within which sensitive personal data about them will be shared, and an assurance that their permission will be sought if those limits are to be exceeded.

There is an issue as to whether therapists who work in private practice outside the NHS are included in the definition of 'health professional' in the DPA exemption from the usual requirement that processing sensitive personal data requires the subjects' explicit consent where 'the processing is undertaken for medical purposes and is undertaken by – (a) a health professional, or (b) a person who in the circumstances owes a duty of confidentiality equivalent to that which would arise if that person were a health professional' (Data Protection Act 1998 Schedule 3 para 8(1)). The DPA defines 'medical purposes' quite closely to mean, in relation to this paragraph, '… preventive medicine, medical diagnosis, medical research, the provision of care and treatment and the management of healthcare services' (Schedule 3 para 8(2)). In the light of this, and of the close definition of 'health professional' in section 69 of the DPA 1998 and the Professions Supplementary to Medicine Act 1960, it would seem that, unless the counsellor is a registered medical practitioner or nurse, clinical psychologist, child psychotherapist, speech therapist, one of the other professionals listed, or a music therapist employed by a health service body, it is unlikely that they will be covered by this exemption.

The second part of the exemption in DPA Schedule 3 para 8(1)(b) refers to 'a person who in the circumstances owes a duty of confidentiality equivalent to that which would arise if that person were a health professional' and we are not aware of any case law that clarifies whether this definition would cover a therapist in private practice.

Points to consider

- Subject to client consent, in principle, therapy notes could form part of shared records held on computer or in written form. Under the DPA, if they include personal data, are processed automatically or as part of a manual 'relevant filing system', or are part of health, education or social services records, they would then be protected by the relevant law, accessible to the client with safeguards, and subject to compulsory disclosure in certain situations required by law (see Chapter 3).
- If a client refuses consent for the therapist's notes to form part of a shared record, the practice or team should have in place a policy and procedure to deal with this situation. Some agencies currently make special arrangements to meet the client's requirements whereas others refuse to offer a service unless the client permits 'shared records' within the agency.
- Consent to disclosure ends the duty of non-disclosure. Consent for disclosure may either be unconditional or qualified in some way. Consent can also be expressed or implied by the surrounding circumstances. Explicit, informed and unconditional consent leaves no avenue of doubt or ground for any subsequent challenge.
- Clients are entitled to make an informed decision and should clearly understand what is being agreed to. Further explanation may be necessary for clarity, especially where confidentiality is explained just briefly and in general terms, e.g. in a GP practice information leaflet.

- If disclosure is required for a purpose other than those specifically agreed with the client, this exception should be explained and the client's explicit consent sought.
- Process notes which identify the client form part of client records. In health, education and social care, client records are automatically subject to the FOIA and obligatory compliance with the DPA. See Chapter 3 regarding DPA regulation of client notes and records.
- Non-identifiable process notes (written in journal form, for example) may escape the requirements for disclosure to the courts or to the people who are the subjects of those records. However, this depends upon thoroughness, because records that the therapist may have intended to be anonymous may nevertheless be accessible by clients and the courts if the client's identity can be inferred or traced from their content, e.g. references to diagnosis, age, family, area where they live, occupation, etc.
- Regarding publications, Pattenden (2003: 435) reminds us that 'doctors who have published data about identifiable patients without first obtaining adequate consent have faced disciplinary proceedings. It is a wise precaution to allow the client to see a final draft of an article before it appears in print'.

Does the therapist have the right to resist a requirement to participate in a shared filing system?

A group practice, team or agency that requires members and employees to share information or records internally (or externally) will need to develop a clear organisational policy and procedures for handling confidential data, understood by all. Chapter 10 explores the development of agency policies and procedures in the context of a counselling service working with Occupational Health in a local authority, with helpful examples.

Points to consider when developing or reviewing policy concerning record sharing

- Do the policies and procedures of the organisation comply with current law? If not, a refusal of compliance may be justified and necessary.
- What commitment to organisational policies and procedures is required by the therapist's contract of employment? Written contracts are helpful for clarity.
- Would a refusal to comply with organisational practice be a breach of the therapist's employment contract? What would be the consequences of a breach?
- For self-employed therapists, what are the terms of their commissioning contract with the organisation? What is the potential consequence of a breach of those terms? For the avoidance of doubt, it is best if the therapist's commissioning contract is in writing, providing clear evidence of the terms of the agreement between the therapist and the agency or organisation.
- Where therapy is directly commissioned and paid for by the client, a clear understanding reached after discussion may then be reflected in a written therapeutic contract providing evidence of the terms of the agreement between client and therapist.
- Therapists working within an organisational setting, for example an Employee Assistance Programme, will have to consider the terms of their contract with the employer or service provider (for example the number of sessions they can offer, boundaries regarding

information sharing, etc.) when negotiating and agreeing the therapeutic contract with each of their clients.

- Whatever personal identifiable information is written down or entered into the computer by the therapist about a client forms part of the client record. Therapists cannot legally keep two sets of notes intending one to be shared and one not to be shared, or withhold all or part of their notes if disclosure of client records is lawfully required.

Therapists considering collaborative practice within multi-disciplinary teams or therapy teams in order to enhance the quality of service being offered

The issues discussed above in the context of working with shared records also apply in this situation, but here we have the added complexity of inter-agency working. Each professional in the team will have their respective professional rules and guidance which may be different from (or even conflict with) those of others in the team. In addition, some professionals may only come together as a team for specific purposes, and individuals may have separate work roles outside the team.

Personal considerations

- Is the team fully aware of and operating within the requirements of the law?
- What is required by the applicable professional disciplinary organisations?
- If more than one professional disciplinary organisation is involved, how compatible are their requirements?
- Does my role in the team conflict at any point with my other roles outside the team?
- Does the team have clear policies and procedures to protect client confidentiality?
- Can I work comfortably within team policies and procedures?
- Are the clients of the team fully aware of and in agreement with the team policies and procedures?
- If difficulties arise and my perception of the best interests of a client conflicts with team policies/procedures, how can we address and resolve this potential conflict?
- What professional guidance is relevant to me and helpful to the team as a whole?

Developments in inter-agency collaboration – the Caldicott Principles

Increasing attention has been given to standards for confidentiality and protection of information, resulting in a large body of what Pattenden (2003: 89–91) calls 'soft law', comprising guidance, departmental circulars, codes of practice, charters, memoranda of understanding and recommendations in departmental and inter-departmental reports. In 1997, the Caldicott Committee delivered the *Report on the Review of Patient-Identifiable Information* (DH, 2006b). That report included recommendations on information sharing within the NHS and between the NHS and non-NHS organisations, embodied in six principles (the 'Caldicott Principles'):

Principle 1 – Justify the purpose(s) for using confidential information.
Principle 2 – Only use it when absolutely necessary.
Principle 3 – Use the minimum that is required.
Principle 4 – Access should be on a strict need-to-know basis.
Principle 5 – Everyone must understand his or her responsibilities.
Principle 6 – Understand and comply with the law.

Caldicott Guardians are appointed to protect patient information in health and social care. They should be existing members of the management board or senior management team, senior professionals, or hold responsibility for promoting clinical governance or equivalent functions within organisations providing health or social care. In 2006, the Department of Health (DH) produced the *Caldicott Guardian Manual* (DH, 2006a) for their guidance. This can be obtained by post or from the websites listed at the end of this book.

The government's intention to annually review and update the *Caldicott Guardian Manual, 2006* is an example of the present intention to encourage and monitor openness in practice. In pursuance of the Caldicott Report, the Department of Health set up the National Confidentiality and Security Advisory Body in the year 2000 and began to develop protocols for information sharing between agencies and organisations, for example in child abuse investigations.

Developments in investigation of child abuse and assessment of children arising from the Children Act 1989 as amended by *Every Child Matters* and the Children Act 2004

The Children Act 1989 was heralded as a radical reform of child care law. The drive for clarity, openness and thoroughness in child abuse investigation has increased since Lord Laming's report on the circumstances surrounding the death of Victoria Climbié, which found that despite the existence of legislation to protect children, there were gross failings in the implementation and management of child protection procedures. The report recommended robust changes in the organisation and provision of child care and protection services at national and local levels, including collaborative inter-agency working across organisational boundaries.

Every Child Matters, a green paper setting out the Government's vision for children's services, was published in September 2003, now implemented in the Children Act 2004. In Scotland, *It's Everyone's Job to Make Sure that I'm Alright*, the report of the Child Protection Audit Review carried out across Scotland, was published in November 2002, and a programme of reforms is now being implemented (see for example the Commissioner for Children and Young People

(Scotland) Act 2003, *Protecting Children and Young People: The Charter* (Scottish Executive, 2004a), and *Protecting Children and Young People: The Framework for Standards* (Scottish Executive, 2004b). Local authorities are empowered to set up arrangements for co-operation among local partners: district councils, police, probation service, youth offending teams, strategic health authorities, primary care trusts, **Connexions**, and the **Learning and Skills Council**, implemented through the **Children's Trust**, with participation by schools, GP practices, culture, sports and play organisations and the voluntary and community sector. These organisations should have clear policies and procedures for information sharing, and therapists working within any of these organisations may be expected to disclose information for the benefit of the child or young person. The Every Child Matters website listed at the end of the book provides detailed online guidance documents dealing with when and how information can be shared legally and professionally. (See *Working Together to Safeguard Children: A guide to Inter-Agency Working to Safeguard and Promote the Welfare of Children* (DfES, 2006c) and its supporting materials, available from the website http://www.everychildmatters. gov.uk. Other useful references are *Information Sharing – A Practitioner's Guide* (DfES, 2006b); *What to do if you are worried that a child is being abused* (DfES, 2006a); and *Confidentiality: NHS Code of Practice* (DH, 2003a)).

In England, the guidance in Part 1 of *Working Together to Safeguard Children* (DfES, 2006c) carries the force of statute under s.7 of the Local Authorities Social Services Act 1970. It sets out the standards and procedures with which local authorities are to comply. The Children Act 1989 (CA 1989) places a statutory duty on health, education and other services to help the local authority in carrying out its functions under the CA 1989. (Similar provisions exist in the Children (Scotland) Act 1995 and *Protecting Children – A shared responsibility: Guidance on Inter-Agency Co-operation* (The Scottish Office, 1998).) There is a statutory duty to work together, including information sharing, in conducting initial investigations of children who may be in need or subject to abuse and in the more detailed core assessments carried out under s.47 of the CA 1989. For details of the assessment process see also DH (2000) *Framework for Assessment of Children in Need and their Families*. Adults and children over 16 or children under 16 but 'Gillick competent' may refuse to co-operate with assessments. In these cases, practitioners concerned for the welfare of the child should refer the matter to the Family Court under the relevant provisions of the CA 1989. The legal department of the local authority may be approached for advice and assistance. See Chapter 11 for a discussion of capacity and consent, including an explanation of 'Gillick competence'.

General points in information sharing

As discussed in the section above, therapists working in organisations will be bound by their contractual responsibilities and relevant organisational policies and procedures. Those working privately must comply with the data protection and human rights legislation, client contracts, statutory demands and overriding

Table 9.1 Disclosure Checklist

It may help therapists in the decision making process about sharing information to consider these points:

- Is this information regulated by the Data Protection Act 1998 (DPA) or the Freedom of Information Act 2000 (FOIA); for example, do the records comprise client-identifiable sensitive personal data held on computer or in a relevant filing system?
- Were the notes made by a professional working for a public body in health, education or social care?
- What are the relevant rights of the person concerned under the Human Rights Act 1998 (HRA)?
- If working in the health community, is disclosure compliant with the Caldicott Principles and Guidance?
- Is there a legitimate requirement to share this information: e.g. statutory duty or a court order?
- What is the purpose of sharing the information?
- If the information concerns a child, young person or vulnerable adult, is sharing it in their best interests?
- Is the information confidential? If so, do you have consent to share it?
- If consent is refused, or there are good reasons not to seek consent, does the public interest necessitate sharing the information?
- Is the decision and rationale for sharing the information recorded?
- What is the most appropriate way to share this information?

---

public interest (where relevant). These, sometimes competing, claims on confidentiality are discussed along with capacity and consent issues in Chapters 3 and 11.

Specific examples of situations where sharing information may be required

Points to consider for a

1   Therapist working in NHS/hospital/GP surgery.
2   Therapist working within private hospital/medical practice.

Therapist records likely to form part of client records. FOIA, DPA, HRA apply. Consider therapist contract, organisational policies, statutory duties, court orders, client wishes and public interest. See the Guidance from the General Medical Council and British Medical Association. Consider the points in the Disclosure Checklist. The Caldicott Principles and the Caldicott *Guardian Manual* are a useful reference for all staff providing health care or social services, and help can be sought from the Caldicott Guardians if in doubt.

3   Therapist in private practice working with client resident in NHS hospital or hospice or otherwise being treated by NHS or other professionals (e.g. PTSD following physical trauma)

Counselling records possibly subject to DPA. HRA applies. Consider therapist's contract employment/consultancy and organisational policies. In all cases, consider statutory duties, court orders, client wishes and public interest. Does client have capacity to consent to disclosure? If information is requested from therapist by NHS professionals, reference to Caldicott Principles may be useful in decision making. Consider the points in the Disclosure Checklist.

4   Therapist providing counselling services in the context of adoption

This is a complex situation. Adoption is an increasingly regulated field in which therapists and others providing counselling services in the context of adoption are subject to the rules on registration of Adoption Agencies. Sensitive information in adoption matters is closely protected by law and the sharing of information is strictly governed by the Adoption and Children Act 2002 and several recent sets of subsidiary rules and the Adoption and Children (Scotland) Act 2007, which is not yet in force.

All registered Adoption Agencies are required to have in place protocols and procedures for safeguarding confidentiality of information, and compliance is compulsory. Useful contacts for advice and resources are the British Association for Adoption and Fostering, and Adoption UK. Their addresses and telephone numbers are at the end of the book, along with the relevant legislation.

5   Coroner requests information from therapist to assist inquest

The role of Coroner is a judicial appointment; therefore a request from the Coroner for disclosure carries the force of a court order, rendering disclosure both legal and compulsory. In case of any difficulty or uncertainty over what ought to be disclosed, it is possible to seek guidance from the Coroner or the Coroner's Officer. This request is best made at the earliest opportunity.

In Scotland, sudden deaths are investigated by means of fatal accident inquiries (see Fatal Accidents and Sudden Deaths Inquiry (Scotland) Act 1976). The inquiry is presided over by a judge, called a sheriff – any order pronounced by the sheriff for production of documents or records is a court order and must be complied with.

6   Next of kin request information from therapist about a deceased client

The present position in the UK is that the legal duty of confidence ends with death, as it is a personal matter, but in equity it is left as a matter of conscience. Therapists will have to form their own view, but may be assisted by their professional organisation's guidance, and by the view of the GMC that a duty of confidence persists after the patient's death.

These points may be helpful in making a decision:

• Did the deceased specifically request certain information to be kept confidential?
• Would disclosure cause distress, or be of benefit to the deceased's partner or family?

- Is the information already public knowledge?
- Could the information be anonymised?

For further discussion, see Mason & Laurie (2006: 292–293).

The Access to Health Records Act 1990 (ACHR) has mostly been superseded by the Data Protection Act 1998, and now only governs access to the health records of deceased people. Copies may be provided upon request and payment of an appropriate fee by the patient's personal representative or any person who may have a claim arising out of the patient's death: see ACHR section 3(f).

7   Mediations where one or both parties is in therapy

Mediation is a voluntary process. Mediators may accept information that is provided by a party to the mediation process by consent, but they have no power to command information from a therapist. If a mediator requests information from client records, therapists should abide by the wishes of their client. If consent is given by the client to share information, it is wise to obtain confirmation of the request and the consent in writing.

8   Therapist working with a client who is also in couple or family therapy

Other therapists may request information from the records of a child client for child protection purposes, in which case disclosure may be necessary in the child's best interests (see the discussion above on inter-agency information sharing under the Children Act 1989, *Every Child Matters* (DfES, 2004a) and the Children Act 2004).

Other therapists may request information about an adult client. If this is in pursuance of a court order, statutory requirement, or necessary in the public interest, then compliance may be required. In all other cases, therapists should abide by the wishes of their client. If consent is given by the client to share information, it is wise to obtain confirmation of the request and the consent in writing.

9   Supervisors of qualified or trainee counsellors
10   Therapists working with counselling trainees as clients

Professional organisations (e.g. BACP, BPS, UKCP) may request information from supervisors on issues related, for example, to accreditation, senior practitioner or fellowship status, or to disciplinary proceedings. This may be a condition of membership to which the counsellor agrees. Training organisations may request information about counselling trainees from their supervisors or from their therapists, either routinely or in cases of necessity on a 'need to know' basis. Some organisations may make this a condition of the training contract.

In both cases, if a request for information is made with the fully informed consent of the client then there should be no difficulty and therapists should abide by the client's wishes, which, for the avoidance of doubt, should be recorded in writing.

If the client objects to disclosure, but the request is made in pursuance of a court order or statutory requirement, or if it is necessary in the public interest, then compliance may be necessary, otherwise the therapist is bound by client confidentiality.

11 Therapist employed or contracted to undertake forensic assessment or direct therapeutic work with client in context of: child protection or private family law case, criminal case, or civil case

If a court order is made for a forensic assessment, court directions made along with the order are likely to govern both the assessment and disclosure of information, i.e. where the examination may take place, who may accompany the person examined, the time frame for the assessment and the person(s) to whom the results should be given. If the client consents to the assessment, obtain confirmation in writing, and comply with the court order. If the client refuses the assessment, do not proceed, but refer the matter back to the court (see Bond & Sandhu, 2005).

10 Developing Agency Policy and Practice — A Case Study*

I have been let down by a lot of people I've trusted at work. It feels like everything I've worked for is just wasted. What I want from this counselling is good professional support, which I think I deserve to get from my employer, and what I need right now is a safe place to start to pick up the pieces of myself.

This client may be expressing the hopes and expectations of many employees who come to a workplace counselling service, and the quotation is a remarkable articulation of the particular qualities they might expect from their counselling. These words hovered in my mind for many months as my team and I developed and wrote a procedure for maintaining client confidentiality and keeping records.

This chapter offers a case study, the development of policy and procedure being a work in progress that remains very much alive and evolving. True to the groundbreaking and frequently changing nature of the law and its application to client confidentiality, we are finding that our application of the procedure, now written, informs further development as our understanding of the issues involved grows, and this speaks also of the nature of the therapeutic work in which we are engaged.

This case study is written from my perspective as manager of a counselling service which is sited alongside occupational health, forming part of the Occupational Health and Counselling Service of Bristol City Council. The study also draws on the views of our team of counsellors and an evolving managerial perspective. As with many workplace counselling services, we have grown organically over the past ten years, from a small number of welfare officers into a team of twelve counsellors, a response to the demand for specialised employee support and growing recognition of the value of therapy. The counselling team comprises very experienced workplace counsellors, with a diverse range of theoretical orientations, including CBT, psychodynamic psychotherapy, Gestalt, solution-focused

This chapter has been contributed by Cindi Bedor writing from her experience as a BACP accredited counsellor, and manager of a counselling service. Her experience in organisational settings includes workplace counselling, managing counselling and multi-disciplinary teams, and policy development. She currently works for the Bristol City Council Occupational Health and Counselling Service.

and integrative therapy. Most of the counsellors work part-time, in a range of venues around the city. Diversity of theory and practice within our team has been valued as a real strength, and over the years the team has tussled with the type and quantity of standardisation to introduce. However, all members of our team agreed that client confidentiality and record keeping processes require standardisation amongst ourselves.

It is a rare thing to feel passionate about policies and procedures, and yet as we immersed ourselves in the process of exploring, questioning, researching and debating every facet of client confidentiality and record keeping practices, some exciting and unexpected things happened: we started talking together about what we really do with our clients, challenging assumptions and well-worn ways of working; at times we trod tentatively around the boundaries that distinguish between individual and collective priorities; we got stuck in our resistances to change; and ultimately we have developed individually as practitioners and also as a team. We started talking to professionals outside our discipline and service, to gain the views of our employing organisation's Legal Services Department, data protection officer and principal insurance officer. We consulted literature produced by the Information Commissioner's Office and BACP, and contacted counselling services similar to ours.

A consultative approach was used in order to incorporate the enormous expertise held within the team and by external professionals. I thank them all for the knowledge and personal contributions they shared freely, and for their patience and persistence.

This case study outlines the process and offers some brief examples of the procedure in action and reflects on the ways in which it has influenced us, our practice and our service. There are probably as many ways of approaching the development of a confidentiality procedure as there are counselling services, and given the few signposts we had at the time to direct us to our destination, our real discoveries have been found in the journey.

Our starting point

When we began, we did not have a written statement or procedure for marking and describing the parameters of client confidentiality and our record keeping practices. Uneasiness was growing amongst our team with each new request for disclosure of information held in a client's file, and this anxiety was fuelled by reports of counsellors being summoned into the witness box. Our discomfort seemed to contain:

- Concern that our clients receive from us a professional service of a high standard on a daily basis, and we would want to maintain this standard in the event that we are called into the courtroom (something that we have not yet experienced).
- Awareness that we assumed we were all working with similar interpretations of our responsibilities regarding confidentiality and record keeping, whilst suspecting that in practice we applied this in different ways.

- Questions about the legal and ethical aspects of our procedures, systems and practice – how will we know if we are working in line with current thinking and good practice? Would they be good enough if put to a legal test? What is really expected of us by our clients, peers, managers, professional bodies, and the law?
- A sense that, due to the workload demands upon us, we were unable to keep pace with the latest research, literature or legal cases regarding confidentiality.
- Anxiety and feelings of vulnerability – who will support and protect us should something go wrong or if we are called to appear in court?
- Concern that the interests and requirements of our employing organisations (also our 'clients') are met.
- A desire to continue raising the standards of our service and our profession.
- Generally a feeling of being lost in the face of a very large and complex issue, not knowing where to begin, and feeling resistant to trying to understand an area outside our training and expertise.

Recently, during a consultation phase prior to writing another procedure, we explored the expectations, needs and requirements of all parties: client, counsellor, supervisor, organisation and profession. The findings of that exercise became the starting point for our discussions about this procedure. A few themes emerged to define our purpose and set the foundation for this procedure: responsibility, accountability, protection and trust. Each party involved in the counselling process required these in some way, and I noticed how frequently the themes were present in our discussions. On reflection now, this exercise laid an essential foundation stone for the development of our procedure. We needed to fully feel, understand and acknowledge the way in which each party held these needs and expectations. It was not enough to simply 'write a procedure'. In addition, we needed to move from assumed to explicit understanding by naming the issues. Finally, we realised that the procedure we wrote must be clear and accessible to anyone, and especially to those outside our profession.

And yet a question remained: how could we be responsible and accountable, offer protection, act in a trustworthy manner and be clear about all of this when each client, and certainly each disclosure request, is different and takes us into unknown, or at least unclear, territory? Our confidentiality procedure must therefore allow a place for unforeseen events and be flexible enough to contain necessary ethical decision-making processes.

Understanding the legal, defensive and managerial issues

We needed to navigate our way through the literature into the realm of confidentiality and the law, which is ever changing and far from our areas of expertise. We were also aware of the current debate and conflicting views regarding note keeping of client sessions, including the use of 'official' and 'process' notes. One view was that no notes should be made; another opinion was that therapists could be deemed negligent if they did not keep notes. Many therapists held the belief that their process notes were their own private property and could therefore contain any material that they believed facilitated their work with their client. Views varied about 'official' notes that are retained in a client's file within an organisational setting, ranging from no notes held to retaining extensive records. Prior to writing our procedure, we fell somewhere in the middle of these opinions by restricting ourselves to noting only the reason for referral, session dates and a brief concluding summary. Each counsellor made and kept their own process notes, of which they held ownership.

Other workplace counselling services, some larger and others smaller than ours, described a wide range of procedures and practice. Most of the services that we contacted had no written procedure but they clearly had agreed working practices, and it was interesting to discover that practitioners in these services believed that they worked to the basic principles of their service procedures while each therapist also applied those principles in their own way, especially so in the making and keeping of process notes. Of the services approached, only one, in another large local authority, had recently written a comprehensive procedure, and this was very helpful to us as a starting point.

Other essential resources consulted at this point included the BACP *Ethical Framework* and Information Sheets, the Data Protection Act 1998, the Caldicott Principles (see glossary and Chapter 6 for definition and further details), and literature and internet searches relating to confidentiality and record keeping.

It was at this point that I contacted our organisation's data protection officer to describe our current practice and seek advice regarding our compliance with the Data Protection Act (DPA) and this dialogue has enhanced collaboration between the counselling service and our employing organisation.

Some key points arising from these conversations were:

1   The issue of a 'relevant filing system' was not pertinent to us, as the case of *Durant v. Financial Services Authority* [2003], which had been widely publicised, does not apply to public bodies such as ours. This meant that we could abandon our early concerns about whether or not we had a 'relevant filing system' and what this meant in practice, particularly when a client requests access to information held about them.

2   Understanding the difference between the Data Protection Act (DPA) and the Freedom of Information Act (FOIA): that the former applies to the collection, processing and storing of personal identifiable information; whereas the latter is mostly concerned with access to non-personal information held by public bodies only. This did raise questions about process notes which were linked to identifiable clients and, in spite of the deep misgivings of some therapists, could be accessed by clients and the courts. There also appeared to be potential problems about anonymised information concerning work with clients, such as case studies and entries in journals, as they could be regarded as non-personal and therefore might have to be disclosed under the FOI requirements for disclosure of information recorded in any form that is not otherwise excluded.

3   Our real challenge, as the local authority data protection officer saw it, was to balance the requirements of data protection; that is, our notes should be 'adequate and relevant' but 'not excessive', and that we should make our decisions regarding our use of process notes by taking both these requirements into account.

In order for the records to be considered 'adequate' all information given to us about a client should be written down and included in the client's file (therefore the client may access the information). In practice, this meant, for example, that the content of a phone call from a manager or other referrer would need to be written in the file and so might later be seen by the client. We considered that we had an obligation to inform the caller of this before they offered us the information. This rightly raised into question a long-held tradition in many workplace counselling services of the 'informal' conversations with a referrer, where information about the client is received by the counsellor but may not always be recorded. Such guidance influenced a change in our practice, and we now advise anyone who wishes to speak with us about our client that we will record the date and content of the conversation in our client's file.

Our clients have a right to refuse to allow us to make and keep notes. Here, we realised our responsibility to give our clients the information that informs them of this right. This raised questions about the ability of very distressed or traumatised clients to understand the implications of this right and make informed decisions, and the sense of responsibility practitioners feel when working with clients at risk, where the concerns and actions of both client and counsellor should be noted. The team also felt ripples of surprise and uncertainty about this challenge to their training, and to the perceived right of counsellors to make notes about their work with their clients. Understanding and validating the great fear and anxiety clients can sometimes bring with them, we did not wish to exclude them from therapy because they exercised their right to refuse note keeping. The dialogue generated by such a refusal is important, and when clients raise concerns about our note keeping, we explore the issues fully with them, explaining the implications of both keeping and not keeping notes of their sessions. We then include a statement on our Confidentiality Agreement Form (a form signed by all clients), that they do not wish us to make or keep notes and that the implications of this have been explained to them. We have yet to be tested by a client we deem at risk, who is clearly telling us they do not want us to make or keep notes. In such a case, our approach of holding the dialogue about it, looking at implications and options, and both client and practitioner exercising their judgement to find a way forward, will play a key role. We continue to consider this issue, in light of practitioners' rights regarding the maintenance of health files, in which they may not be required to gain explicit client consent to make notes or records of sessions as a result of an exemption in the DPA where 'the processing is undertaken for medical purposes and is undertaken by '(a) a health professional, or (b) a person who in the circumstances owes a duty of confidentiality equivalent to that which would arise if that person were a health professional' (Data Protection Act 1998 Schedule 3 para. 8 (1)). Given the definitions in the DPA and other legislation discussed in Chapter 9 coupled with the absence of any case law to clarify this issue, it is still unclear whether those working outside the NHS would benefit from this exemption.

4   A preference for a confidentiality statement to be given to the client, ideally signed by the client, and retained in the client's file with the notes.

It was increasingly apparent that our next task was to reach a balance, if possible, that would fulfil the legal requirements of the DPA, and the ethical and professional obligations of our professional body, BACP. Now with a greater understanding of the DPA, I approached our Legal Services Department and our professional practice insurer to gain guidance on meeting legal requirements, and what they would need should they ever be in the position of defending a counsellor.

The legal team provided a guideline on the minimum amount of data to hold, preferring more rather than less information. Points arising from my discussions with them included: whether our client files should be considered 'health records'; the issue of informed consent; the requirement that data held electronically and on paper are treated in the same way in terms of what is retained and for how long; and what exemptions may be requested by a counsellor if a court requests client information that a counsellor considers potentially harmful to the client or another party.

Our principal insurance officer's view was that, for defence purposes, as much information as possible is preferable and that contemporaneous information, written immediately or as soon as possible following each counselling session (rather than days or weeks later), is most useful in evidence in any court or tribunal.

Our consultation process also included senior managers in our organisation. Of greatest importance to them, in addition to adherence to the law and relevant organisational policies, was that the expectations and parameters integral to the counselling process are offered, in written form, to clients at the outset of their counselling. The purpose of this was to inform employees of what they can expect of counselling, what is expected of them, and what to do if they are unhappy about the service they have received. A client/counsellor contract was suggested, to include a confidentiality agreement and an outline of our client's rights under the DPA.

Decisions that have shaped our procedure

Many thoughtful discussions led to the following decisions.

We would consider our client files as 'health files'   This was a management decision, to acknowledge the setting within which the Counselling Service operates, to promote consistency within the entire occupational health and counselling team, and to facilitate partnership work with occupational health colleagues where appropriate. Further advice was sought from the Information Commissioner's Office regarding health records. It recommended that we undertake an impact assessment, a tool created by the Information Commissioner's Office to assist employers to weigh up the benefits and any adverse impact of collecting and using employees' information. The tool facilitates identification of the purposes for collecting information, any likely adverse impact of collecting and holding the information, whether there might be any alternatives to this, what obligations exist and whether the collecting of information is justified (Information Commissioner's Office, 2005). This was a very useful process to undertake and it confirmed the conclusions we had already reached.

To adopt a recording system to retain information on a client's file   This would include:

- Name and contact details
- Date of referral
- Date of birth
- GP name and address (to facilitate prompt liaison with the GP where the client is particularly vulnerable or at risk)
- Reason for referral
- Dates of sessions
- A brief summary of the content of each session, including assessment; or whether sessions had been cancelled or not attended
- A concluding assessment

To keep separate process notes and if they are either general (non-specific to a particular client) or not an essential part of a specific client record, they are shreded one month after the counselling sessions end   To meet the requirement of the DPA, we were advised to destroy the process notes within a reasonable time, one to two months following the end of the therapy. We chose to shred them after an interval of one month to allow sufficient time for the counsellor to take the process notes of their work with the client to their next supervision session.

To improve information given to clients, potentially at all stages of the counselling process, but especially at commencement of counselling   This would now include (in addition to a counselling leaflet and other practical information previously given):

A Confidentiality Agreement, which outlines to clients what they may expect from counselling, the parameters of confidentiality; what to do if they are not happy with their counsellor, and practical aspects such as cancelling an appointment.

A Guide to Data Protection, describing what information is held and how it is obtained, for what purposes it is used, how it is cared for and for how long, and what clients' rights are in relation to the information held about them, including the right to require us to hold no personal data about them.

A counselling agreement signed by both client and counsellor. This was reluctantly accepted by counsellors, but was recommended by other parties in the consultation process. In practice it increased the potential of a perceived authoritarian tone in the counselling room, which felt at odds with the ethos and practice of therapy. It also called into question the issue of informed consent, and many of our very vulnerable or traumatised clients may not be in a position, at the outset of therapy, to give informed consent. We ultimately chose to change the agreement to a tick-box form, signed by both client and counsellor, to indicate that the client had been given verbal and written information about confidentiality and data protection.

This was also a place to record the names of anyone they wished to be included in the confidentiality agreement, either at the outset of counselling or later, if agreed.

To ensure that all notes of sessions are contemporaneous   That is, preferably written immediately following the session or, if that is not possible, within the following two days at most.

To keep files for seven years following the conclusion of counselling, unless exemptions apply   Exemptions would include the client returning to counselling, the client having a period of mental incapacity, or any other reason the therapist (on behalf of the organisation) may have to retain a file for longer.

To contemporaneously document all actions taken   This includes: all verbal and written communication; all decision making processes and outcomes or actions taken; dated and initialled by the counsellor who is documenting. This is to facilitate an accurate representation of what has happened in relation to the client, and why, and to improve duty of care on behalf of the organisation to the client (e.g. should the client's counsellor suddenly become unavailable to work, duty of care continues as best as it possibly can for the client).

Our decisions were made but we remained uneasy. With no real awareness and experience of the different legal processes, or being 'tested' by a client complaint or disclosure request for an inquest, how do we know that we have done enough, or made the 'right' decisions? We remained concerned about retaining some flexibility in order to be able to use our judgement and expertise; about how to enter into an ethical decision making process openly and with integrity; and how to present the need for some flexibility as necessary to therapeutic excellence. Accountability for decisions made (or not made) rests much more heavily upon managers' shoulders than practitioners', and I was acutely aware of the enormous expectations of all stakeholders, and that managers – myself included – would be held to account in the event of something going wrong. As a manager and at the interface between the therapeutic work of our service and other external professionals, I became increasingly convinced that therapists cannot assume that other professionals will understand or comply with the principles, values, mechanisms and language of therapy. It is therefore our responsibility as therapists to value, articulate and protect both the known (theoretical and ethical frameworks) and the unknown (within the therapeutic encounter) in our work. This requires the use of our judgement and decision making processes.

Our client files procedure has therefore been prefaced with the underpinning framework of: the Caldicott Principles; the relevant points of the Data Protection Act 1998 and the BACP *Ethical Framework for Good Practice in Counselling and Psychotherapy (2007)*; and a statement about the complex and controversial nature of client confidentiality and note keeping, the potential for the therapist (with the collective agreement of their supervisor, manager and professional body) to use their judgement and to work outside of this procedure if necessary, and the aims and intentions of the service to provide safety to clients alongside an awareness of the needs of all parties.

The procedure written, forms were developed and training provided to counsellors and others directly involved with the counselling service. Overall, it was a lengthy process, partly due to the consultative approach that encouraged the counselling team to make and own as many decisions as possible, and partly to a lack of definitive, tested guidance in the areas of confidentiality and record keeping.

The influence and impact of this procedure on our professional development and our practice

The greatest influence of this procedure upon our practice is in our contracting with clients; we now more clearly and comprehensively outline what they may expect from their counselling, what confidentiality means in practice and what exceptions apply, that we keep notes and how we do this. We have found that clients are more comfortable with our tick-box form than they – and we – were with signing an agreement, and that we have more fruitful discussions about what confidentiality means to them within this setting.

A few clients have refused us permission to keep notes, but have agreed to sign the form stating they have received the confidentiality and data protection information. In these cases, we have documented on the form their stated wish to have no notes made of their sessions. This feels a difficult agreement to make, as the potential exists for the counsellor to be disadvantaged, possibly unfairly, in a legal, or indeed organisational process, and it is a point we hope to further define and reconcile.

Conversations between counsellors and referrers (managers or human resources) now include the advice that the content of the conversation will be noted in the client's file, to which the client may have access. Much to our surprise, this seems to have had little impact upon our relationships with referrers.

Other difficult questions arose amongst us, concerning what we were holding on to and why, whose interests were being served, and if or when there might be occasions when extensive notes should be retained. Each counsellor writes client notes, including process notes where appropriate. Some of the counsellors' process notes may be either general (non-specific to any particular client) or intended for temporary use by the counsellor, for example for use in personal reflection in their supervision. In the context of current legislation, the challenge for our counsellors now lies in identifying whether all (or part) of their process notes should be retained as part of the client record. Any process notes that do *not* form part of the client record will be shredded after a month.

An interesting concept has come to me through this process, which I have termed 'the life of the file'. It is a realisation of just how much the paper file reflects the life of the therapy – perhaps not in terms of therapeutic dynamics and interventions, though in some cases, such as child protection or other areas of risk, it will involve noting decisions and interventions, but more related to the 'activities', e.g. correspondence, attendance and cancellations, and the 'framework' within which it all takes place. By framework I mean the agreements, intentions and understandings we are working to at this point in time, recognising that the framework may change over time, and if a client returns at a later date, the agreements to which we work may be different, and those agreements or parameters would then become part of the file. To support this concept, we now include in the client's file a copy of the Confidentiality Agreement, the Guide to Data Protection, and the signed tick-box form along with the session notes. These documents are dated, and retained in an order, to represent a picture of the parameters within which we were working at that time. This also helps to maintain a higher duty of care standard for clients, should another counsellor need to see them in the future. My belief now is that a client's file deserves the quality of attention and level of responsibility that is invested in the therapeutic process. From a manager's perspective, attempting to create systems that stand in their own right, when staff come and go over the years, my challenge is to develop and embed this awareness within counsellors, who often view the administrative aspect of counselling as unecessary, uninteresting and irrelevant, and who are unaccustomed to creating files and records as if their clients or other parties will see them.

Of great value to our team during this process have been the discussions and debates, all of which have rewarded us with glimpses of each other's beliefs and practices, previously assumed, and have led us to a better understanding of where we work in similar ways and where we diverge. At times this has felt risky and has mirrored a shared fear of external eyes interpreting and judging one's practice. We have further embedded a systemic view of our role within a large organisation, and the needs of each party involved. Alongside this have come new collaborations with our data protection officer, solicitors and principal insurance officer, which we hope to build upon as we regularly review and update this procedure.

It was hoped, at the outset, that counsellors would feel more confident and less fearful of being called to account for their work, with a written procedure in place. Although understanding of the legal and ethical responsibilities has increased, and our systems and practice are more efficient and professional, the hoped-for confidence has increased little. It was made very clear to us that we must make our own decisions about our procedure, based upon the varying opinions available to us. We remain acutely aware that in a field where our judgement is crucial in our daily encounters with clients, the judgement of others involved in processes with which we are unfamiliar, who have agendas of their own, and do not understand the values and mechanisms of therapy may hold much greater power than our own. However, it occurs to me that we are able to support ourselves by having a written procedure in place that states our intentions and our limitations in accordance with clear legal guidance, legitimising the need to use judgement and ethical decision making processes and representing the therapeutic work in a legal, ethical and fair way through our documentation and contemporaneous notes held in our clients' files.

Reflections and conclusions

To have a written procedure for client confidentiality and record keeping in place, and one that is meaningful to us, feels a great achievement and a relief. The process has been lengthy: nearly ten months from the outset of our discussions to the implementation of the new procedure.

These reflections by some of the counsellors represent some of our struggles and achievements.

> *The process made me realise what a minefield it is to develop a client file procedure within an organisation as large and complex as a local authority. It seemed an impossible task to come up with something that would satisfy the legal, insurance and ethical requirements and yet still not stifle us as counsellors in our creative practice with clients. Even though I was anxious about how the changes would work in practice, it feels as though we have adapted to the new way of working very well. I also feel more secure now in the knowledge that how we record has been scrutinised and considered at great length.*

> *Awareness of recording has influenced what I write, why, and to whom, during the counselling process, consciously observing a new discipline of self. To work towards accuracy, answerability and responsibility, which is influencing the systems we, the client and I, work in. It also impacts on the recording mechanisms of other departments in our organisation. I have started to experience a new freedom that has enabled me to feel that the client, the counsellor and the organisation are working in unity.*

> *I didn't initially feel comfortable with the additional contracting paperwork as part of the first session, and I feared it would inhibit clients who want to talk as soon as they come through the door. But what I find is that by going through the confidentiality agreement more thoroughly, a dialogue is opened up, we are engaged in a shared activity and it all feels much clearer for both of us.*

> *Originally I was unconvinced that it was important to have a set order of the file as long as it was complete. However, I feel the new client file format has had a much deeper effect on the way I feel about how this material is held and recorded. Somehow, with the extra clarity and a comprehensive system, it does feel that more respect is being expressed for the material and the work between the clients and ourselves. It is more pragmatic, but also impacts on a psychical level.*

One of the most enlightening aspects of this process has been the presence of strong emotions that have arisen as therapists' ways of working have been called into question by the Data Protection Act and the increase in litigation. I have frequently noticed a tension and movement between confidence and anxiety: as beliefs and assumptions about confidentiality and note keeping were made explicit; as therapists began to write their notes 'as if' their client – or a court – were reading them; or as we realised that, despite all our expertise and our efforts to produce this procedure, there remains no guarantee that our notes will be seen by others as we intended when we wrote them.

Throughout the process I have noticed what seems to be the personal nature of note keeping to each practitioner, and how much meaning this has to them, a testament to a firmly protected relationship between therapist, client and notes. Our decision to make process notes and shred them after one month was a way of honouring the importance and life of that relationship, and this is something a court of law may never understand about our work.

It was probably not surprising, then, to sense the ripples of shock as the reality of the changes required were absorbed: 'How can my training and practice over all these years be wrong?' 'How can I make these changes and still feel I'm practising as well?' The anxiety raised here needed to be heard and enough time allowed for discussion, support and reassurance. This may have been one of the most fruitful steps towards understanding and accepting what have been, for some therapists, fundamental changes in their practice.

Our paperwork relating to the procedure continues to evolve, frustratingly at times, as I search for the best way of representing the integrity of the therapy in the file and also meet therapists' needs for straightforward administrative processes. However frustrating, this does ensure that our discussions continue. Each time I read again the key documents underpinning our procedure, I gain more insight into other possible interpretations and applications for our work with clients and this generates further refinements in the procedure. There is more clarity to be gained for us in the way that confidentiality and note keeping apply to counselling files that are considered health files, and we may implement changes as we begin to understand these issues.

Old habits die hard, and we still catch ourselves as we slip into well-worn ways of working or forget to document a phone call. For the most part, practitioners are now more at ease with the changes they have made, and as a result our contracting with clients is clearer, and our files are more consistent and cogent.

The process of developing a procedure for client confidentiality and record keeping has brought many achievements: we have found some degree of balance that we hope meets the needs and rights of all parties, at least at this point in time; we have sharpened our awareness of our responsibilities and accountabilities; we have found consistency in this core aspect of therapy while retaining our theoretical differences; we better understand each other and the work we do; we are more rigorous practitioners; what we previously held as assumed knowledge about these issues is more explicit, and we are more respectful. Surely our clients deserve and will benefit from this.

From a manager's perspective, it has been a rewarding opportunity to work with such an open and skilled team of counsellors and managers, to build new relationships within the organisation, to further the understanding of counselling with other professionals and gain their support, to improve the clinical governance of our service, and to begin to meet the legal and professional challenges of our time. We are far more aware of the changing interface between the therapeutic encounter, confidentiality, record keeping and the law, and the increasing challenges to practitioners to integrate the concept of accountability into their practice.

Our current procedure is far from exhaustive and definitive, and will continue to evolve as we become more familiar with the principles, laws and interpretations that inform it. My sense is that our procedure is heavily weighted towards fulfilling our data protection responsibilities; and that this may be at the cost of the therapy. With increasing complexity in our casework, we may choose to retain more case notes, either process or file notes, to keep the consistency and integrity of the therapy intact. Perhaps our greatest achievement is that we have begun to engage with these issues and principles, and we are more open to meeting future changes in the law and our profession.

As therapists working in organisations, we must actively address these cultural and organisational challenges. We are skilled at holding our confidence in the midst of the unknowns of the therapy; and we may also need to learn how to find such confidence in the face of unknown legal and organisational processes.

11 Mental Capacity, Parental Responsibility and Consent

He brought the baby for his immunisation jabs. He said that he was the baby's father so he could give consent … but I was worried whether he had the right …

She left home at 16 and came for counselling. She said that I was to tell no one about the abuse by her father, but I was worried because her younger sister is 11 this year and she might be the next one now that her sister has left home …

He was 14, but very bright and spiritual and he had strong religious beliefs. He wanted to decide for himself whether to have a blood transfusion, and he was adamant that he did not want one. His mother believed that his immortal soul would be in danger if he was given the blood. His father wanted him to have the transfusion as he believed that the sickle cell anaemia would kill his son otherwise.

She was seeing pixies running behind the coal scuttle last time she came to see me … surely there is no way she could be able to make a will?

She was eight months pregnant. She went into hospital after a road accident, and they did a Caesarean without her consent … when she regained consciousness she was furious …

I was working with a 13-year-old lad, and we were getting on very well in the counselling. He can't speak very well, but I understood him and felt that he was beginning to trust me, then one day his mother came in and said that I was to stop working with him …

Working with a client's consent is one of the best ways of solving any problems over confidentiality or record keeping. For most adults who are capable of understanding the issues and expressing their wishes, this is a relatively unproblematic area of law and practice. The law will generally protect an adult's right to make autonomous decisions for themselves. However, therapists are often working with people who may be distressed or experiencing some impairment to their normal functioning or with children and young people who have not reached legal adulthood. In this chapter we will consider the ways in which mental impairment or other legal limitations might prevent a client from giving a valid consent to receiving therapy, and who can give valid consent on the client's behalf when this is required. A client's ability to give legally valid consent to any medical, psychiatric or therapeutic assessment or treatment, or to enter into either a valid therapeutic contract or a legally binding contact for services, will depend upon their mental capacity to make an informed decision.

Mental capacity

Mental capacity is a legal concept, according to which a person's ability to make rational, informed decisions is assessed. It is presumed in law that adults and children over the age of 16 have the legal power to give or withhold consent in medical and health care matters, provided that they have mental capacity. This presumption is rebuttable, for example in the case of mental illness. A refusal of necessary medical or psychiatric treatment by young people over the age of 16 but under the age of 18 may be overruled by the High Court/Court of Session (more of this later).

Currently, the legislation has made a transition from the Mental Health Act 1983 (which had some serious gaps regarding consent) to the comprehensive new legal provisions embodied in the Mental Capacity Act 2005, the Mental Health Act 2007 and the Mental Capacity Act 2005 (Appropriate Body) (England) Regulations 2006 SI. 2006 No. 2810. Relevant publications and websites are listed at the end of this book. For the relevant provisions as they apply to Scotland, see the Adults with Incapacity (Scotland) Act 2000 and the Mental Health (Care and Treatment) (Scotland) Act 2003.

There is no single test for mental capacity to consent. Assessment of mental capacity is not on a theoretical ability to make decisions generally, but is situation specific and depends upon the ability of the person to:

- Take in and understand information including the risks and benefits of the decision to be made
- Retain the information long enough to weigh up the factors to make the decision, and
- Communicate their wishes.

Part 1 of the Mental Capacity Act 2005 (MCA), which came into force on 1 October 2007, defines 'persons who lack capacity' and sets out the principles underpinning actions taken under the Act, including a checklist to be used in ascertaining their best interests. In particular, it requires that a person is not to be treated as lacking capacity simply because they may be making an unwise decision.

A person may be mentally incapacitated on a temporary basis (i.e. unconscious in hospital after an accident), or on a longer-term or permanent basis (i.e. those who suffer from severe long-term mental illness or other impairments of mental functioning) and in their case, the capacity to make medical decisions is likely to be assessed by a medical doctor or psychiatrist. The assessment of a person's mental capacity for other tasks may be made by others: for example the decision on their capacity to make a will may be made by a lawyer; or the decision on whether they can engage in therapy may be made by the therapist. If there is any doubt, advice from an appropriate registered medical practitioner, psychiatrist or psychologist should be sought. If there is a dispute about a person's mental capacity to make an important medical decision, the matter should be referred to the High Court/Court of Session, which will then assist and, if necessary, make a ruling.

Consent

A person's capacity is relevant in therapy when dealing with issues of consent, especially when considering whether someone can give a valid consent to receive therapy or agree the terms on which therapy is being provided. Capacity to give a valid consent may depend upon a number of factors, notably:

- For what action is consent being sought?
- Have all the potential benefits, risks and consequences of taking or not taking that action been fully explained and understood?
- Has the person retained the information long enough to properly evaluate it when making their decision?
- Can the person clearly communicate their decision (with help as appropriate) once it is made?
- Is the consent sought for the individual concerned, or is it for the treatment of another person?
- If consent is sought for another person, is that person an adult or a child?
- If consent is sought for a child, does the person giving consent have parental responsibility for the child?

Consent for another person to act/make decisions on behalf of a vulnerable adult

On occasions, therapists may be in doubt as to whether a client can give valid consent for the therapeutic contract or therapists may need to determine issues regarding confidentiality and disclosure of information, for example consent from another person may be necessary before engaging in therapeutic work with young people, children or vulnerable adults.

Therapists may be asked to work with vulnerable adults and to assist them to consider all the relevant issues in making difficult decisions, for example in family relationships, or when considering treatment or long-term planning for their future care. The therapist may need to work alongside or in co-operation with health care staff and others. Adults in residential care may also wish to take advice from specialist professionals, e.g. lawyers, financial advisers, in making decisions about their property or financial affairs. Some adults will have intermittent mental capacity to make specific decisions. Adults who do not have the mental capacity to make their own decisions may need others to give consent to sharing information, medical or psychological treatment, or for the day to day running of their affairs. The Court of Protection protects and manages the property and financial affairs of people with impaired mental capacity. The Public Guardianship Office provides administrative support for the Court of Protection. In Scotland, a similar role is fulfilled by the Office of the Public Guardian in terms of the Adults With Incapacity (Scotland) Act 2000.

An adult with mental capacity (the Donor) can appoint another person to act as their Attorney to run their affairs. These appointments may be made either with immediate effect, or contingent upon a future loss of mental capacity. Under earlier legislation, the donor could create an *Enduring Power of Attorney*, limited to running financial and property affairs: sources of information, forms and relevant websites are listed at the end of this book.

However, this is a fast developing area of law, and on 1 October 2007 the Mental Capacity Act 2005 (MCA) came into full force, replacing the previous legislation. The MCA creates the new *Lasting Power of Attorney*. The major change is that the donor will not only be able to appoint an Attorney to carry out duties relating to property and financial affairs, but in addition, the Attorney can be empowered to make decisions on the health and welfare of the donor, including giving or refusing consent for medical treatment or therapy in circumstances where the donor has lost the mental capacity to do so for himself. The Lasting Power of Attorney must be registered under the Court of Protection Rules 2007 immediately it is to be implemented. Information, forms and guidance from the government are available on the websites and addresses listed at the end of the book. For Scotland, see sections 15 and 16 of the Adults With Incapacity (Scotland) Act 2000.

'Advance directive', 'advance statement', 'living will' or 'advance decision'   Therapists may be asked to assist clients in developing plans or expressing their wishes for present or future health care arrangements. While they have mental capacity, some clients may wish to make an 'advance directive' (otherwise known as an 'advance statement' or 'living will') about the forms of medical treatment to which they may (or may not) consent if they should subsequently lose the capacity to decide for themselves. Advance directives refusing treatment are legally binding, provided that they are made while the person had capacity, without duress, and that the circumstances to be applied are clear. Sections 24–26 of the MCA empower those who wish to do so to make 'advance decisions' concerning their wish to refuse specified treatment.

There are conditions under the new MCA:

An advance decision is not applicable to life-sustaining treatment unless:

(i)   the decision is verified by a statement to the effect that it is to apply to that treatment even if life is at risk, and (ii) the decision and statement comply with these rules:

    (a)   it is in writing,

    (b)   it is signed by the person or by another in their presence and by their direction, the signature is made or acknowledged by the person in the presence of a witness, and

    (c)   the witness signs it, or acknowledges his signature, in the person's presence.

There are legal provisions in the MCA to limit the types of decision that can be made by an Attorney, to safeguard against misuse of advance decisions, to appoint mental capacity advocates and visitors, and to prevent the neglect or mistreatment of people with mental incapacity. See also the Adults With Incapacity (Scotland) Act 2000 and the Mental Health (Care and Treatment) (Scotland) Act 2003. Further information, the full text of the MCA, the Court of Protection Rules 2007 and government guidance are available from the organisations and websites listed at the end of the book.

Consent: children and young people under the age of 18

Therapists working with children and young people will need to have valid consent to enter into the therapeutic contract. The legal issues surrounding work with children and young people are complex because of the need to provide services for children in need, and to protect children from abuse. There is an emphasis in current law and practice on inter-agency co-operation in working together to safeguard children. Please refer to Chapter 9 for further discussion of information sharing between professionals. All too often, professionals do not have sufficient understanding of the law regarding consent in relation to working with children and young people, for example making the erroneous assumption that all parents can make medical and therapeutic decisions for their children. As a result, therapists and other professionals may inadvertently act without appropriate legal consent. This section seeks to clarify the law in this field.

A child is defined in law as a person under the age of 18 (CA 1989 s. 105 and the Children (Scotland) Act 1995, s. 15(1)). 'Parent' is usually interpreted as meaning the biological mother and father or adoptive parent of a child, but in some legislation the term may include other people who are not the biological parents but have parental responsibility for the child.

People may assume that all parents have the power to make decisions for their children. This is emphatically (and perhaps surprisingly) not so. The ability of a parent, or anyone else, to make a decision for their child depends on whether they have 'parental responsibility', which is the legal basis for making decisions about a child, including consent for medical treatment.

Parental responsibility

The Children Act 1989 (CA 1989) created the concept of 'parental responsibility', defined in section 3(1) as 'all the rights, duties, powers, responsibilities and authority which by law the parent of a child has in relation to a child and his property'. Note that there is new legislation under consideration which may change and further define the concept of parental responsibility. See also the Children (Scotland) Act 1995, s. 1. More than one person can have parental responsibility for a child at the same time. It cannot be transferred or surrendered, but aspects of parental responsibility can be delegated, see the CA 1989 s. 2(9), Children (Scotland) Act 1995, s. 3(5)).

Mothers and married fathers   Every mother (married or not) of a child born to her, and every father who is married to the child's mother at the time of or subsequent to the conception of their child, automatically has parental responsibility for their child, which may be shared with others, but will be lost only by death or adoption.

Unmarried fathers   Unmarried fathers may acquire parental responsibility for their biological child in one of several ways, the first three of which can only be removed by order of the court:

- In England, from 1 December 2003, an unmarried father automatically acquires parental responsibility for his child if, with his consent, he is named as the child's father on the registration of the child's birth. This law does not operate retrospectively. For Scotland, see the Family Law (Scotland) Act 2006, s. 23.
- By formal 'Parental Responsibility Agreement' signed by the mother and father, witnessed by an officer at court, then registered. Copies may be obtained for a fee, in a similar way to obtaining a birth certificate: see Parental Responsibility Agreement Regulations S.I.1991/1478 and the Children (Scotland) Act 1995, s. 4.
- A court making an order awarding parental responsibility to him, consistent with the interests of the child.

Parental responsibility can also be acquired by a child's biological father through:

- Parental responsibility awarded along with a residence order directing the child to live with the father.
- Appointment as child's guardian (operates when appointment takes effect after the death of the appointer).
- Marriage to the child's mother.
- Adoption of the child.

Acquisition of parental responsibility by others Parental responsibility may be acquired by others in a variety of ways.

- Adoption. In this case, the parental responsibility held by all others prior to the adoption will be lost.
- The child's mother may enter into a parental responsibility agreement with her civil partner (subject to the agreement of the father if he has parental responsibility) (CA 1989 a 4A (1) as inserted by ACA 2002 s. 112 and amended by CPA 2004 s. 75 (1).
- The civil partner of a mother may seek a parental responsibility order from the court (CA 1989 a 4A (1) as inserted by ACA 2002 s. 112 and amended by CPA 2004 s. 75 (1). In Scotland, the civil partner may seek an order under section 11 of the Children (Scotland) Act 1995.
- The child's father (if he has parental responsibility) may enter into a parental responsibility agreement with his civil partner (subject to the agreement of the child's mother) (CA 1989 a 4A (1) as inserted by ACA 2002 s. 112 and amended by CPA 2004 s. 75 (1).
- The civil partner of a father with parental responsibility may seek a parental responsibility order from the court (CA 1989 a 4A (1) as inserted by ACA 2002 s. 112 and amended by CPA 2004 s. 75 (1).
- Step-parent adoption by the civil partner of the mother of a child born through assisted reproduction (HFEA 1990 was not amended by CPA 2004).
- A parental order under s. 30 HFEA 1990 declaring a married couple to be the parents of a child born through surrogacy arrangements. This order operates like adoption, and the child's surrogate birth mother loses her parental responsibility.

In the other situations listed below, parental responsibility may be acquired and shared with those who already have it in relation to the child, but the exercise of parental responsibility may be limited by the court in various ways.

Parental responsibility may also be acquired through:

- Residence order awarded by the court (s. 8 and s. 12 CA 1989), s. 11 C(S)A 1995.
- Guardianship (CA 1989 s. 5), s. 7 C(S)A 1995.
- Care order made under s. 31 CA 1989 (parental responsibility is acquired by the local authority) see CA 1989 s. 33 (3), s. 86 C(S)A 1995.
- Emergency Protection Order (but the duration and exercise of parental responsibility is limited).
- Special guardianship.

There is an additional provision in section 3 (5) of the Children Act 1989 that those without parental responsibility may 'do what is reasonable in all the circumstances to safeguard and promote the welfare' of a child in their care, for example allowing a babysitter or relative to take a child in their care for medical help in an emergency, see also s. 5 C(S)A 1995.

Medical or psychiatric examination, therapy or assessment of children

A distinction must be made at the outset between examinations and assessments for diagnosis and treatment including therapy, and those purely for forensic (court) purposes.

Examinations for diagnosis or treatment (including therapy) of children

What constitutes valid consent in law for medical examination or treatment of a child or young person under the age of 18?

- Consent of a person with parental responsibility for the child.
- Consent of the child, if aged over 16 (under the Family Law Reform Act 1969 s. 8 (1), Age of Legal Capacity (Scotland) Act 1991, s. 1).
- Consent of a child aged under 16, if they have sufficient age and understanding of the issues involved and the consequences of consent (i.e. the child is 'Gillick competent' as defined in the case of *Gillick* v. *West Norfolk and Wisbech Area Health Authority and Another* [1986], Age of Legal Capacity (Scotland) Act 1991, s. 2 (1) and (4).
- A direction of the High Court/Court of Session.

General (non-emergency) treatment   Consent will be required from a person with parental responsibility for a young child; and if an older child of sufficient age and understanding is competent to make his own medical decisions, the therapist may also accept consent from the child. Any kind of physical examination carried out without such consent could render the practitioner liable for assault in civil or criminal law, or both.

Emergency medical treatment   If this is medically required and there is grave risk to the child if emergency treatment is not given, practitioners may rely on their own clinical judgement if those in a position to give consent are unavailable.

Treatment is necessary but no consent   If a practitioner considers assessment or treatment necessary and consent is not forthcoming from any of those entitled to give it, the High Court may use its powers to act in the best interests of a child under 18, authorising the requisite assessment or treatment as lawful. If a problem arises concerning consent, the legal department of the local authority or health service, and professional organisations, may provide advice and assistance, and a direction may be sought from the High Court, if necessary using the 'out of hours' court service for emergencies.

What if those with parental responsibility refuse, but the child consents?

- If the child is over 16 or 'Gillick competent' – the child's consent is valid.
- If the child is not 'Gillick competent' – the child's consent is not valid. If examination or treatment is advised, obtain legal advice and if necessary a court order may be sought. The High Court will make an order if it is in the best interests of the child and the parents' consent is being unreasonably withheld.

What if those with parental responsibility for the child disagree with each other?

- If the child is over 16 or 'Gillick competent', and the child consents, this is valid, and can be accepted.
- If the child is not 'Gillick competent', the child's consent is not valid. If examination or treatment is advised the parties in disagreement should obtain legal advice and, if necessary, they may apply to the court to resolve their dispute with a 'Specific issue' order made under section 8 of the Children Act 1989/section 11(2)(e) of the Children (Scotland) Act 1995.

What if a child refuses a medical examination, assessment, treatment or therapy?
A young child (i.e. under the age of 16 and not 'Gillick competent') cannot give a valid consent, nor therefore a valid refusal. If there is any issue about the competence of the child to make an informed decision, this issue can, if necessary, be referred for expert opinion and/or to the High Court.

A child over the age of 16 has the right to refuse medical examination or treatment, see the Family Law Reform Act 1969 s. 8 (1), but in some situations the High Court may overrule their refusal (see below).

A child under the age of 16 has a similar right of refusal if they are of sufficient age and understanding to understand their circumstances and the potential benefits and risks of the treatment proposed to make an informed decision. They must have an understanding of the issues, including the risks and benefits involved and the consequences of refusal, i.e. the child is 'Gillick competent' as defined in the case of *Gillick* v. *West Norfolk and Wisbech Area Health Authority and Another* [1986].

In the case of *Re W (A Minor: Medical Treatment)* [1992], Lord Donaldson, supported by Lord Balcombe, said unequivocally, 'No minor of whatever age has power, by refusing consent to treatment, to override a consent to treatment by someone who has parental responsibility for the minor, and a fortiori a consent by the court.' In *Re L (Medical treatment: Gillick competency)* [1998], Lord Donaldson reiterated that position, adding that nevertheless, such a refusal is a very important consideration in making clinical judgements and for the parents and the court in deciding whether themselves to give consent.

The High Court will make decisions in situations where doctors (or those with parental responsibility) face dilemmas. If a child over 16, or 'Gillick competent', has a diagnosed clinical need for treatment but refuses to have it, despite those with parental responsibility for the child having given their consent, if the doctors feel that the proposed treatment is medically necessary, but feel that in all conscience they cannot (or should not) proceed against the child's wishes, legal advice may be sought and the matter referred to the High Court, which is empowered to make a decision in the best interests of a child under the age of 18 and may then, after considering all the circumstances, declare the proposed medical treatment to be lawful.

Once a person reaches maturity, i.e. 18 years of age, even the High Court cannot overrule their wishes about medical examination, treatment or therapy unless for any reason they lack the mental capacity to make their own decision. Note the provisions of the new Mental Capacity Act, under which a 'deputy' may be appointed by the Court of Protection to make health and welfare decisions for another adult who does not have the mental capacity to make their own decisions.

Control by courts of examinations of children for purely forensic (court) purposes

Therapists may be asked to carry out an assessment of a child or young person and possibly also to provide a report and attend court to give evidence. In the case of child protection, or family conflict, for example care proceedings or contested contact matters, one or more of the parties may disagree with the assessment and require a second opinion. Repeated medical and psychiatric examinations for forensic purposes can cause a child unnecessary stress. The Children Act 1989 and the Children (Scotland) Act 1995 and their subsidiary rules empower the court within the context of court proceedings including emergency protection, child assessment, interim care, and care or supervision applications, to regulate such examinations and make appropriate directions, which may nominate the practitioner(s) to carry out the examination or assessment, the venue, those to be present, and those to whom the results may be given. Breaches of these rules are viewed seriously, and the court has power to disallow any evidence obtained without compliance with the rules.

The child's right to refuse forensic examinations and assessments   A child of sufficient age and understanding may make an informed decision to refuse a forensic examination or assessment, even if it has been authorised by the court. A child's ability to refuse will depend on factors including age, understanding and the information given. Practitioners should ensure that a child who is competent to make a decision is given an explanation appropriate for their age of what is proposed and the potential consequences of refusal. A note should be made of the information given to the child and of the substance of the questions and answers on which the practitioner's assessment of the child's capability to make decisions is based. That note may later be required in court if the child's capability is questioned.

In care, supervision, child assessment and emergency protection proceedings brought under the Children Act 1989/Children (Scotland) Act 1995, a Children's Guardian/Principal Reporter should be available to assist the court in ascertaining the child's views and advising the court on the best interests of the child. When a child is brought to a doctor or therapist for a forensic examination or assessment in accordance with a direction of the court, but then refuses to comply, the examination or therapy should not proceed, but the matter should be referred back to the court.

Having considered the capacity of clients to give consent, we will now follow up the information in the book at a practice level. In the next and final chapter, we explore the ways in which we might manage the practical challenges of negotiating confidentiality and recording confidences.

12 Recording Confidences: Practical Guidelines

In this final chapter we provide some practical guidance on how to respond to the legal responsibilities created by the current law with regard to respecting clients' confidences and record keeping.

Identify your policies on record keeping and confidentiality

Most therapy services delivered by groups of therapists or within organisations will have developed written policies and protocols in order to co-ordinate service provision. Sole practitioners do not need to consider the challenges and opportunities of working with colleagues but may still benefit from thinking through their policies with regard to clients in order to inform their negotiations and agreements with clients. There are no general legal requirements to have written policies but where they exist they may be used as evidence to support claims to be working to professional standards. However, they may also be used to challenge the appropriateness of a policy or to investigate the extent to which a policy is being applied in practice.

Major issues concerning record keeping and confidentiality with potential legal implications are:

- Determining the levels of confidentiality offered to clients and who has access to that information as being included within the 'circle of confidentiality'.
- Communicating to clients the degree of confidentiality being offered to them and whether a record of any agreements over confidentiality ought to be kept.
- Identifying processes for responding to exceptional cases that may fall outside routine practice or are especially challenging.
- Ensuring that keeping any records of sensitive personal data is based on the client's explicit consent.
- Keeping any records securely.
- Determining the purpose(s) for which records are kept and for how long, and that this is compatible with clients' consents.
- Ensuring that the terms of any contracts of employment for therapists and other staff or for the provision of services, including supervision and training, are compatible with these policies.

Policies and protocols create a general framework for delivering services but are not usually legally enforceable until they are incorporated within specific agreements and contracts between the people affected. Where there is a conflict between a policy and an explicit agreement between two parties, for example client and therapist or employee and employer, the law will tend to enforce the explicit agreement. The two exceptions to the law enforcing an explicit agreement are where this would conflict with statutory law or would be contrary to the public interest, for example by preventing the investigation or detection of serious crime. This makes the compatibility between practice and policy a major concern for both managers and practitioners in therapeutic services. The compatibility between agency policy and what is offered to clients is a critical concern for any service. High compatibility will usually provide the best basis for providing a professional service that clients can trust and also provide the best protection for therapists and others from legal liabilities. Incompatibilities create tensions within any service that may lead to successful claims against that service or create conflicts of responsibility and liability for the staff concerned.

Managing client expectations

There are many reasons why a therapist should be concerned to ensure that their clients have appropriate expectations of what they are being offered. Professional ethics for therapists emphasise respect for client autonomy and being trustworthy, which requires that clients are appropriately informed about what is being offered to them and that the therapist is watchful for potential misunderstanding. Managing clients' expectations so that they know what to expect in advance helps to create the circumstances in which clients feel safe enough to face the challenges of receiving therapy. It may also increase their level of satisfaction with the service on offer and should help to prevent dissatisfaction reaching the level that prompts litigation or formal complaints.

Any concerns over confidentiality and record keeping will usually be raised in discussion between the therapist and client and therefore both parties need to share their understanding of what has been agreed and their memory of that agreement. In many circumstances this is unproblematic. However, the lack of any evidence of what has been communicated can become problematic if a client considers that they have been misled or harmed in any way. If there are no records of the outcome of the discussion, there is often no way of satisfactorily establishing what occurred in the event of any dispute. It is just one person's word against another. If the disagreement escalates into a legal dispute over confidentiality, the law operates in ways that will generally favour a client claiming a right to confidentiality. The legal presumption in favour of regarding therapy as confidential is so strong that in the absence of any evidence to the contrary, a court will imply a term of confidentiality and hold a therapist liable for a breach of the terms created and implied by the court within any legally enforceable contract. Similarly, claims for breach of confidence in common law and under data protection will start with an assumption of a commitment to confidentiality unless the therapist can establish a legal exception based on the client's consent, a statutory duty or the balance of public interest. This means that therapists are legally wise to ensure that clients are informed in advance of any exceptions to confidentiality and that any issues that appear to be significant to either client, therapist or agency are adequately recorded in ways that could be produced as evidence.

In this section, we will set out some of the commonly used practices that help to manage clients' expectations. These practices support the therapeutic relationship as their primary purpose but can also provide useful evidence in the event of dispute.

- *Pre-therapy information*: Typically pre-therapy information may be provided in advertisements for services, on posters, entries in directories, web pages or in leaflets. All of these are both potential sources of information for clients and evidence of the terms on which therapy is being offered. It is reasonable to promote a service as 'confidential' if this is what is intended and to provide further information about any limitations of confidentiality to potential clients before they commence therapy. Claims to provide 'absolutely' or 'totally' confidential services are legally unwise as the law may require disclosure of information and in some circumstances refusal to do so may result in fines or imprisonment for contempt of court or breach of a statutory duty. Therapists making such claims are facing themselves with a choice between honouring their promise or taking the consequences of offering more than the law will countenance. Some clients will seek further information about a service by correspondence or informal conversations with the therapist. These exchanges may also contribute to establishing the legal basis of the service provided to the client and it is wise to keep a record of any variations from usual practice concerning confidentiality that have been offered to clients.
- *Evidencing the legal basis for confidentiality and record keeping*: A client's explicit consent is usually required for any communication of confidential information about them and to make records of personally sensitive information concerning the client. Oral consent is sufficient but consent that is evidenced in writing by signature and date provides the best quality evidence. Where this is not possible or desirable, a note in a case record made as close as possible to the time of the consent is the next best evidence.

Therapists vary in their practice in how they obtain the explicit consent and establish evidence that a client has given consent.

- Leaflet, and file note made by the therapist that the client has received the leaflet and agreed to receive services on this basis. In the event of a dispute, a client may deny that they gave consent as there is only the therapist's word for it.
- Leaflet, and signed consent form in which the client agrees to receive therapy on the terms set out in the leaflet. As in the previous arrangement, the leaflet becomes in effect the terms of the contract but the client provides evidence that they agreed to these terms by a signature.
- Letter of engagement setting out the terms on which therapy is provided with a provision for the client to provide a signature on a duplicate copy or reply slip. Examples 12.1 and 12.2 provide examples of how the terms for providing therapy can be set out. Example 12.1 is presented as a series of rights and responsibilities for both therapist and client. Example 12.2 is structured around setting out the services offered to clients, how the services will be provided, and the client's responsibilities. Both these examples assume that confidentiality is held within the therapist–client relationship. They can be

modified where confidentiality is held by an agency; where records are shared across agencies; or where therapy is provided in services that actively seek to involve the client's carers – an approach which is currently being promoted in mental health (Institute of Psychiatry and Rethink, 2006).

During the course of researching and writing this book we have found that there is a great variety of practice in how therapists manage the expectations of their clients. Most therapists attempt to strike a balance between attempting to be explicitly comprehensive so that every possible circumstance in which a therapist might be legally or ethically obliged to compromise confidentiality is covered, however unlikely, and providing something that is more user friendly for clients, based on more frequently encountered issues. Some therapists are concerned to provide the basis of their agreement with clients in ways that avoid intimidating them by formal legal contracts, or meeting the needs of those who struggle with written documents because of literacy or language difficulties. Some therapists working with people with learning difficulties use pictures as prompts to discussions about their client's expectations of the basis on which therapy will be provided. Although the law directs attention to the importance of a client's informed consent concerning the management of confidentiality and record keeping, it does permit a great deal of flexibility in how this consent is obtained and evidenced.

Example 12.1   Agreement based on rights and responsibilities

Client rights and responsibilities

In counselling, both the Counsellor and the Client have rights and responsibilities. It may be helpful for you to read these few notes before we begin our session together and to clarify any concerns you may have about coming for counselling before we start.

As a client you have certain rights. You have a right:

1   To dignity as an individual human being. You have the right to equal consideration and treatment regardless of your sex, race, religion, colour, economic status, age, sexual preference or beliefs.
2   To be provided with professional and respectful care by your counsellor.
3   To be accepted as you are, and to be listened to in a non-judgemental way.
4   To know your counsellor's assessment of the problem or concerns that you are presenting.
5   To refuse to comply with recommendations, even though your counsellor may strongly suggest you take some form of action or seek some other form of help. You may choose not to follow the counsellor's guidance. Alternative resources may be available and you have the right to know what these are.
6   To confidentiality within counselling, subject to the law or if there is the risk of serious harm to yourself or to others. You should also know that your counsellor is bound to comply with the Ethical Framework for Good Practice of the British Association for Counselling and Psychotherapy.

(Continued)

(Continued)

Along with these rights you have certain responsibilities. These are:

1   To be honest, open and willing to share your concerns with your counsellor.
2   To ask questions when you don't understand or when you need clarification.
3   To discuss any reservations you have about your future options with your counsellor.
4   To report changes or unexpected events with your counsellor as related to your problem.
5   To keep appointments or to give at least 24 hours advance notice when you need to cancel or reschedule an appointment and to pay the agreed fees to the counsellor.

You are responsible for your own thoughts, feelings, actions, and for your own personal growth. Your counsellor is here to help you to help yourself, to the best of your abilities.

As your counsellor I may wish to keep notes of our work together and discuss the counselling that I am doing with you with my supervisor, in order to monitor and improve my practice. This will be done in such a way as to protect your identity and to protect your confidentiality. I would be grateful if you would confirm that you have given me permission to do this.

Signed...Date..

Signed...Date..

Example 12.2   Agreement for the provision of therapy by [insert agency or therapist's name]

The services offered to clients

Counselling/psychotherapy provides you with an opportunity to present issues that are causing you concern, difficulty or distress to someone who is [offering]/[trained and experienced in providing] psychological and relational help. [This service specialises in …]

As your therapist I will respect you as a person and endeavour to honour your trust. I will respect your confidences and protect them from disclosure to others unless authorised by yourself or by law.

I am a [type] member of [professional body] and bound by their ethical framework and code of conduct.

How therapy will be provided

At the end of the first session, we will discuss what is likely to be most helpful to you and how you want to proceed. Sessions are arranged by appointment, last [xx] minutes and cost £[xx]. If I consider that some other form of therapy may be more beneficial to you I will recommend that type of therapy and will try to assist you in obtaining it.

If I consider that you are at imminent risk of causing serious harm to yourself or others, I may seek additional assistance on your behalf or on behalf of vulnerable others. This will normally be done with your consent unless the circumstances prevent this, in which case I will, where appropriate, endeavour to inform you about what has been communicated and to whom. You are recommended to let me know of anyone from whom you wish to receive additional support [and with whom I may communicate on a confidential basis] between sessions should this be required.

In order to enhance the quality of therapy being offered to you, I may discuss my work with you on a confidential basis with colleagues and my therapeutic supervisor. Records of sessions will be kept securely up to [x months/years] after your last session, and then they will be destroyed. Records may be 'weeded out' periodically to remove information that no longer serves a therapeutic purpose and does not form part of a brief factual record of our work together.

Any communication of information about you for research or professional development requires your explicit consent. Your refusal to give consent will not affect the service you receive.

Your responsibilities as a client

- To communicate as openly and honestly as possible.
- To ask about anything that is unclear to you or causing you concern.
- To attend and pay for appointments promptly, giving no less that 24 hours' notice of any cancellations.
- To communicate any changes in circumstances that might impact on your therapy.

****

I agree to these terms for the provision of therapy:

Client's signature: Therapist's name

Date: Date:

Record keeping

This section sets out the types of material that could be included in clients' records that would assist with the management of confidentiality and be consistent with the legal requirements concerning keeping records that contain sensitive personal data. If the records are kept on paper in a way that follows the subheadings in this section, they will amount to a structured manual file and therefore be subject to the Data Protection Act 1998. Therapists working in public authorities need to be mindful that their clients may obtain access to both structured and unstructured files following rights granted under the Freedom of Information Act 2000.

The content and structure of files varies between therapists. The suggested structure that follows has been chosen to assist the setting out of associated legal issues but there is no legal reason why the sections should not be re-ordered, combined, or omitted according to the requirements of the type of service.

Contact details   These include name and address as well any means of communication between sessions, for example to change an appointment time or to follow up a missed appointment. Some clients may prefer not to be contacted at home and others may wish to avoid communications at work. The accuracy of these contact details is important because misdirected mail containing sensitive health information has resulted in substantial payments to patients as out of court settlements for breach of confidentiality.

Additional sources of support for vulnerable clients   Therapists vary considerably in whether they require this type of information but, if this information is collected, clients should be informed about the circumstances in which these contacts might be used. Client consent to the therapist making contact with additional sources of support eliminates legal difficulties over confidentiality. A decision by a therapist to override an adult client's explicit refusal to permit communications with others about the client, however well intended by the therapist, requires legal justification such as a statutory duty or the balance of public interest. Additional sources of support might include the client's medical doctor, family, friends, carer or an organisation known to either the therapist or the client.

Referral details and any communications with referrer   These records might include notes of oral referrals, letters, or completed referral forms as well as any communications to the referrer to report progress.

Agreement with client about terms and conditions of providing therapy   The purpose of this section is to demonstrate that the client's consent has been obtained and the terms and conditions on which the consent has been given. This section could include a signed agreement or a copy of the information provided to the client about the type of service being offered; notes of any variations to standard terms; and notes of any legally required assessments of a client's capacity to give consent, especially if the client is a child, a young person or a vulnerable adult.

Records of sessions   Typically records of sessions are organised chronologically and include the date; duration and locations if these vary; a factual summary of issues raised by the client; the therapist's responses especially any advice, guidance or 'homework'; and notes of any therapeutic assessments, interpretations, or plans for future interventions. Therapists who keep process notes vary in whether these notes are integrated into the records of sessions or kept in a separate section within the client's notes. Some keep any process notes in a separate document such as a journal or preparatory notes for supervision. These notes are part of the client records for legal purposes if the client is identifiable by name or if the client's identity can be inferred from the circumstantial details. Records that only contain the therapist's subjective processes in which clients are not identifiable probably cease to be part of the client's record for most purposes. However, this does not mean that they will be totally protected from a client's right of access (less likely) or a requirement to disclose as part of litigation (a remote possibility but more likely). There is a clear tendency in decided cases to favour professional accountability over respect for the professional's privacy but we have not found any decided cases that precisely determine when a record is too remote to constitute part of the client's record. This would be decided on the circumstances of the case.

Example 12.3   Case note – Part 1: Client work

Client reference (optional)

Date

Venue

Length of session

Events/issues arising between sessions

Client's issues in this session

Assessments, therapy plans/interventions

Therapeutic responses/advice or guidance given

Homework

Future plans/issues to be addressed

Date, time and venue of next session

Additional notes:

Records of consultations about client with others   These notes include records of discussions with colleagues, supervisor, service manager, and any other sources of therapeutic support and record any outcomes of these consultations, for example recommendations or plans. They should include any discussions with members of the client's family or other contacts as it is this type of discussion that is most likely to raise concerns over confidentiality for the client. This would be the appropriate place to record any disclosures of confidential information (possibly cross-referenced to the session notes, see Example 12.3) including to whom information has been disclosed, the content of the disclosed information and the basis on which it was disclosed, such as with client consent or other legal justification, giving reasons for doing so. Where legal or professional advice has been sought about the management of the case, especially issues of confidentiality, this would be the obvious place to include a record about seeking advice and the content of the advice received. This might also be the place in which to include any correspondence and notes of any telephone calls received or undertaken concerning the client not included elsewhere.

Example 12.4   Case note – Part 2: Professional consultations and information shared with others

Professional consultations (e.g. colleagues, supervisor, service manager)

Issues addressed

Recommendations made

Disclosures of confidential information

Date

Recipient

Disclosure made orally/in writing

Information given

Correspondence/telephone calls	**Date**	**Brief content**
Client's explicit consent to disclosure	yes/no	written/oral
Client's implicit consent to disclosure	yes/no	written/oral
No consent:	Brief reasons for disclosure	

Records kept separately from the client's file   Some records may be kept separately for the practical reasons that they are of a different size from the file or require a different form of storage, for example, notes made during sessions on flipchart paper; clients' notes or drawings made during sessions, and any real time recordings of sessions e.g. audio or visual recordings. Some records are best kept separately from the client's records in order to protect their privacy and confidentiality. A diary of appointments is likely to require frequent consultation and is one of the few instances where records concerning most or all of the clients using a service are combined. People who require access to an appointment diary will not necessarily require access to the client's full notes. Any financial records of payments are also best kept separately from the individual client records so that they can be administered and audited separately from the therapy records, for example to complete tax returns or manage resources.

Once records of confidential or private information have been created about identifiable living people a number of legal obligations follow. These obligations exist regardless of length, format or how the records are structured. There is a strong ethical obligation to keep the records securely and protected from unauthorised intrusions or use. This ethical obligation is legally reinforced by statutory obligations about data protection. If there are no applicable statutory obligations, common law requires that confidential records are adequately protected.

Anyone who makes therapeutic records should be aware that there is always the possibility of clients obtaining a legal right to see their records and that any record may be required to be disclosed as evidence in legal proceedings. It is not always possible to anticipate when these legal obligations will arise so it is best to consider that any record, however trivial or substantial, may be subject to a client's access rights or required by the courts.

Managing the tensions in recording confidences

There is an inherent contradiction in recording confidences that troubles therapists. The contradiction is substantially the result of the way the law treats records. The law requires that clients are legally entitled to access their own records, subject to certain conditions and exemptions. Perhaps more problematically, records may also be required to be disclosed in legal proceedings which may result in all or part of them becoming public knowledge, contrary to confidentiality and the professional ethic emphasising client privacy. Since the publication of the first book in this series we have spoken to hundreds of therapists from around the British Isles, many of whom are uneasy about the way the law appears to require exposure of what has traditionally been regarded as private to therapy. Sometimes the therapists have failed to appreciate the distinction between clients' rights of access to any records held about them and the processes by which records may be subject to 'discovery' as part of litigation. In this final section we will revisit some of the recurrent questions that have been put to us as we discussed the experience of therapists.

What ought to be the general attitude to keeping therapeutic records?

Most lawyers with whom we have discussed this topic have recommended starting to answer the question by identifying the purpose of therapy and asking: how could that purpose best be achieved for the client? Issues of confidentiality should probably be regarded as secondary and many of them can be managed by involving the client in the decision-making process. Therapists appear to be less sure that this is the case. They share the concern of acting in ways that are best for clients. Typically they strive to manage confidentiality and record keeping in ways that assist the delivery of the highest possible quality of therapy. However, some therapists may be working with clients who are too fearful or paranoid to tolerate the keeping of any records. In some cases, the clients may be too ill to have mental capacity. Other clients unwilling to tolerate the keeping of records may have mental capacity but also suffer from excessive fears or simply be unwilling to allow disclosure of any part of their records; or they may feel too vulnerable to prejudice or stigma to want to risk the existence of records. These fears may be an issue to work with within the therapeutic alliance, or on which a negotiated compromise agreement may be reached, provided that the therapist is mindful of ethics and is able to act within the terms of agency policies and/or their employment contract.

In some settings it may be impossible to provide a reasonable level of security for any records. The sense of order and reason that characterises much of the law may not be compatible with the realities of working with marginal groups on the edge of society because of mental illness, poverty or intolerance. This is where deciding the purpose of therapy as the basis for informing policy and practice may lead to different conclusions from the general run of therapy but this does not invalidate the general approach to confidentiality which we outline in this book. In most instances the law operates as a general and loose-fitting framework that can accommodate variations in practice provided the therapist works within that framework and can explain why they have adopted particular policies and practices. Although the *Ethical Framework for Good Practice in Counselling and Psychotherapy* (BACP, 2007: 5) states that 'practitioners are encouraged to keep appropriate records of their work with clients unless there are adequate reasons for not keeping any records', there is no general requirement to keep records or to retain them for any specified period. However, therapists should bear in mind the issues and circumstances outlined in Chapters 6 and 7 when deciding whether records are required and how long to keep them. It may be appropriate to weigh the benefits of keeping records against the deterrent effect on potential clients or the difficulties in keeping the records securely. Therapists may also need to consider carefully their own or their agency's/organisation's general policy on record keeping – for example, is it appro-priate to maintain a policy to keep records for most clients but to make exceptions for certain other clients for reasons which the therapist or agency may consider justifiable? Similarly the data protection requirement that clients should give explicit consent to the keeping of records allows considerable variation in how that consent is obtained and does not require that it is evidenced, although it would be wise to do so. The mere existence of a legal requirement ought not to shut down professional considerations of how to meet the require-ments in ways that meet the circumstances of the service and the needs of clients.

How does the law approach granting clients a right of access to most therapeutic records held about them if the clients' reaction is likely to destroy the therapeutic relationship?

This question appears to be based on assumptions that have been changed by recent developments in contemporary culture, professional ethics and the law. All citizens have been granted much greater access to records of which they are the subject in order to give them the opportunity to correct any records and to know what is being communicated about them. This means that records can no longer be regarded as of exclusive concern to the professional who made them. Nor should they be separated from the therapeutic process. Records and record keeping should now be regarded as integral to the therapy. The best way of guard-ing against the possibility of records having a detrimental effect is by considering the content of records as they are compiled and how a client might view them. Other ways of minimising any potential damage to the therapeutic relationship may include offering to be present when the client views the records or persuad-ing the client to defer access to a more suitable time. Where viewing the records could be detrimental to a client's health there are limited opportunities to deny access, as outlined in Chapter 6.

A therapist who is unduly anxious about a client seeing his records may need to reflect on her own practice and motivation in supervision and if necessary with professional advice. The anxiety may be appropriate to the circumstances. However, it may be disproportionate and indicate that, although the therapist has genuine concerns for the client, it also stems from the therapist's concerns for her own welfare or unease about some aspect of her therapeutic work. She may fear that if the client should see his records she will lose the client or that something in the records will provide evidence for a complaint. These anxieties may be helpful prompts to review and develop practice or enhance professional support.

Does the law recognise the client's rights to privacy concerning matters discussed in confidence within therapy or contained in the records?

This is not an issue for clients' access to their own records as this takes place with-out breaching their privacy or confidentiality. It is an issue for the discovery of evi-dence for litigation. Courts will generally favour obtaining any relevant evidence that will enable them to decide cases as reliably and fairly as possible even if that means overriding someone's rights to privacy. A client who is choosing to com-mence proceedings may wish to balance concerns over the privacy and confiden-tiality of their therapy against the potential benefits they are likely to gain from the case. They have much less control where they are subject to cases initiated by others. Like any party to a case, they may challenge the use of evidence on the grounds of its relevance, perhaps for consideration by a judge prior to the hearing. (For further information on this see Bond & Sandhu, 2005.)

Does the law recognise a therapist's right to privacy concerning their subjective experiences when delivering therapy?

The answer is generally 'no'. The law views clients' access rights to their own records as a basic civil right that arises and exists for as long as records concerning an identifiable and living person are in existence. This right is strongest where records fall within the terms of the Data Protection Act 1998. If the therapist includes private personal information within the record then the client would usually have access to this because it forms part of that record. (This is different from the rights of third parties who have a degree of protection for information that they have provided within the record: see Chapter 3.) It follows that therapists should only include in a client's record private or personal information about themselves if they are willing for a client to see it. For example it may serve a therapeutic purpose to consider the therapist's reactions to the client as projections or counter-transferences and it would be hard to avoid some disclosure of the therapist's psychological processes that in other circumstances might be regarded as private to the therapist. Similarly, where the therapist shares a similar experience to the one that the client is presenting in therapy, it may be important for the therapist to set out and examine the two experiences in order to distinguish resonance (which may beneficially assist and inform therapeutic empathy) from over-identification with the client's experience (which may work to the detriment of the therapy). In many situations clients would probably be reassured by knowing that these issues have been attended to. However, if the therapist considers it inappropriate to address these issues in the case notes, they could be addressed without reference to the specific client in a professional journal or in notes for supervision. These notes would not usually need to be shown to a client under their rights of access provided that the identity of the client cannot be inferred.

The reasons that apply to disclosing documents as evidence in litigation are different, but lead to a broadly similar outcome. The principle that guides which parts of any client record may be required for disclosure in litigation is their relevance to the case – a fact which can only be determined by the lawyers representing the parties to the case or by the judge. It is hard for someone outside the legal process to anticipate what might be considered relevant because it depends on interpretation of the records and construction of the case.

As therapy is an interpersonal and intersubjective process, it is arguable that taking on this role does mean that therapists risk exposing their psychological processes because their relevance is so much greater than would be the case in a largely physical form of intervention such as surgery or dentistry. If this line of reasoning is correct, then exposure of personal material is an occupational hazard best considered at the time of taking up the role or deciding whether therapy is an appropriate vocation. A therapist who tries to defend their personal privacy after working with a client may be too late to do so.

Will keeping records increase the probability of therapists being required to give evidence?

This question is usually asked by therapists who regard giving evidence, whether written or oral, as outside their expertise and an unwelcome extension of their role. These fears, particularly in relation to a specific case, can usefully be considered in the context of supervision, as they may simply stem from fear of the unknown – i.e. the courtroom process – in which case this can be addressed by discussion with a lawyer, visiting a courtroom in advance for familiarisation, or by training; or they may stem from the therapist's self-doubts or some level of anxiety about the therapeutic work which would benefit from discussion in supervision.

Therapists understandably might want to minimise the possibility of being caught up in legal proceedings. However, the answer is not quite as straightforward as the question, nor is it entirely consoling to these reluctant witnesses. The experience of therapists of being caught up in legal proceedings is that the absence of records may eliminate relatively superficial involvement in a case where the therapy was considered to be of very little relevance to the case. On the other hand a lack of records may create the circumstances for a much more demanding involvement in the case if the therapy is considered to be highly relevant. An absence of records is contrary to the usual expectations of professionals and therefore may be questioned and challenged by lawyers. Lawyers tend to ask for notes as a matter of routine. When receiving a lawyer's request for notes, a court report can be offered instead. In some cases, ascertaining the relevant issues from the lawyers and client, and then addressing the salient issues in a court report prepared by the therapist with the consent of the client, may provide what the court needs and if the report is accepted by all parties, it may obviate the need for the therapist to give evidence. The lack of records may prevent the therapist from providing evidence by submitting any available case notes or compiling a report from those notes. Therefore, it could make it much more likely that the therapist will have to give evidence in person. This is probably the outcome that therapists who ask this question most want to avoid. Keeping records might have provided them with some degree of protection from giving evidence in person, but cannot provide total protection.

This fear of giving evidence may be better addressed by getting adequate training. It may also be that the profession collectively needs to review its basic training or continuing professional development in order to prepare its practitioners better for providing evidence. It does appear that litigation requiring evidence from therapists is becoming a more frequent occurrence. Any therapist working with suicidal clients, people who have suffered physical injury due to an accident or assault, or clients with work concerns, family separations or criminal behaviour, will have a reasonable chance of being required to provide evidence. For some this will be a relatively low chance but we also encountered services, such as those working with the victims of sexual abuse or rape, where giving evidence has become an integral part of the work.

The subject of this book has raised issues of law as well as how the law is applied and impacts on the work of therapists. It has brought us into contact with both lawyers and therapists, some of whom have dual qualifications. Our overall impression is that there are some inherent tensions in recording confidences disclosed in therapy but many of these can be reduced by discussion in supervision, being better informed about the legal requirements and processes and anticipating how records might be used while they are in existence. Confidentiality and privacy will remain central concerns in therapy because of the real or perceived sense of vulnerability of clients to being exposed to others. Here the law is helpful to many clients because it strengthens clients' right to confidentiality in most circumstances. However, the right is not absolute and, as in ethics, there may be times when there are more pressing concerns, particularly for the good of society as a whole, that may override an individual's rights. The therapist is best placed to respond to these situations by being as well informed as possible in advance and adapting their policy and practice to comply with the current law. This assists the management of any dilemmas but cannot entirely eliminate the difficulty or unease experienced by clients and therapists. Actively involving clients in decisions about their privacy and confidentiality provides the best way of resolving most situations. However, there will always be some situations which cannot be wholly resolved by informed consent. Often these are situations where respect for a client's autonomy is eclipsed by the demands of fairness between people and justice.

Glossary

These are brief explanations of some of the most important terms used in this book. For further details please refer to the relevant chapter.

Anonymised data Data from which the client cannot be identified by the recipient of the information. The name, address and full post code must be removed together with any other information which, in conjunction with other data held by or disclosed to the recipient, could identify them. Unique numbers may be included only if recipients of the data do not have access to the 'key' to trace the identity of the client.

Caldicott Guardians are appointed to protect patient information in health and social care. They should be existing members of the management board or senior management team, senior professionals, or hold responsibility for promoting clinical governance or equivalent functions within organisations providing health or social care. In 2006, the DH produced the *Caldicott Guardian Manual* for their guidance.

Caldicott Principles Six principles for testing whether to disclose patient-identifiable information as part of recommendations on information sharing within the NHS and between NHS and non-NHS organisations: see the *Report on the Review of Patient-Identifiable Information* (DH 2006b) by a committee chaired by Dame Fiona Caldicott in 1997 (the Caldicott Committee).

Circle of confidentiality A group of people sharing confidential information with the client's consent, for example a health care team, or a counselling organisation with group supervision.

Client records Generic term which includes all notes, records, memoranda, correspondence, photographs, artifacts and video or audio recordings relating to an identifiable client , whether factual or process related, and in whatever form they are kept.

Clinical audit Evaluation of clinical performance against standards or through comparative analysis, to inform the management of services. Studies that aim to derive, scientifically confirm and publish generalisable knowledge constitute research and are not encompassed by the definition of clinical audit in this document.

Competent adult   A person aged over 18 and mentally capable of giving valid consent.

Confidentiality   A wide ranging duty of managing information in ways that keep it secure and control its disclosure. It is concerned with protecting information that is identifiable with a specific person, typically because the person is named, but the law will also protect the confidences of people whose identity can be deduced from the available information, perhaps because the listener knows some of the circumstances of the person being referred to. Thoroughly anonymised information in which the identity of specific people cannot be discerned is not protected by the law of confidentiality.

Data   Defined in section 1 (1) of the Data Protection Act 1998 to mean information held about a person which is processed automatically, is part of a relevant filing system, or is part of an accessible record. Data may therefore include: computer-based records and certain manual records, tape, video and audio recordings, laboratory results, notes, memoranda etc.

The term 'Data' otherwise denotes a collection of statistical or other information gathered in the course of research. (Also see **personal data** and **sensitive personal data** below.)

Data controller   Defined in section 1 (1) of the Data Protection Act 1998 to mean a person who (either alone or jointly or in common with other persons) determines the purposes for which and the manner in which any personal data are, or are to be, processed.

Data processor   Defined in section 1 (1) of the Data Protection Act 1998 to mean any person (other than an employee of the data controller) who processes the data on behalf of the data controller.

Data subject   Defined in section 1 (1) of the Data Protection Act 1998 to mean an individual who is the subject of personal data.

Duty of confidence   A duty of confidence will arise whenever the party subject to the duty is in a situation where he either knows or ought to know that the other person (about whom he holds information) can reasonably expect his privacy to be protected.

Explicit consent   Term used in the Data Protection Act 1998 to mean consent which is absolutely clear and specific about what it covers, i.e. not implied by surrounding circumstances. Explicit consent may be given orally, but for the avoidance of doubt, it is always best to have it confirmed in writing wherever possible. Wherever the DPA refers to explicit consent in a record, then it must be in writing. See the Data Protection Act 1998 – Legal Guidance at http://dataprotection.

gov.uk. The NHS Guidance interprets explicit consent to mean 'signed consent with no ambiguity and a full statement of the purposes for which it was given.' See http://www.ssimg.freeserve.co.uk/Guidance/managing_personal_data.htm

Express consent   This involves active affirmation, which is usually expressed orally or in writing. If clients cannot write or speak, other forms of unequivocal communication of consent may be sufficient.

Forensic   In general terms, forensic simply means court-related, i.e. a forensic report is one ordered by the court or prepared for use in court; forensic evidence is evidence used in court cases, etc.

Health care team   The health care team comprises the people providing clinical services for each patient and the administrative staff who directly support those services.

Implied consent   Agreement which is inferred from circumstances. For example, implied consent to disclosure may be inferred where clients have been informed about the information to be disclosed and the purpose of the disclosure, and that they have a right to object to the disclosure, but have not objected.

Incompetent adult   A person aged 18 or over and who lacks the mental capacity to give valid consent.

Mental capacity   A legal concept, according to which a person's ability to make rational, informed decisions is assessed. It is assumed in law that adults and children of 16 or over have the mental capacity and therefore the legal power to give or withhold consent in medical and health care matters. In Scotland, Section 1 (1)(b) of the Age of Legal Capacity (Scotland) Act 1991 provides that a person of 16 years of age or over has legal capacity to enter into any transaction, which includes medical and health care matters. Section 2 (1) provides that a person under the age of 16 can consent to a transaction of a kind commonly entered into by persons of his age and circumstances and on terms which are not unreasonable and Section 2 (4) specifically provides that a person under the age of 16 years shall have the legal capacity to consent to any surgical, medical or dental procedure where, in the opinion of a qualified medical practitioner attending him, he is capable of understanding the nature and possible consequences of the procedure or treatment. These presumptions and rules are rebuttable, for example in the case of mental illness. A refusal of necessary medical treatment by young people over the age of 16 but under 18 may be overruled by the High Court (or Court of Session in Scotland). There is no one test for mental capacity to consent. Assessment of mental capacity is situation specific, and will depend upon the ability of the person to take in, understand and weigh up information including the risks and benefits of the decision to be made, and to communicate their wishes. See Chapter 11 for further details.

Parental responsibility   The legal basis for decision making in respect of children under the age of 18, created by the Children Act 1989 and defined in section 3 (1) as 'all the rights, duties, powers, responsibilities and authority which by law the parent of a child has in relation to a child and his property'. It is possible that the definition of parental responsibility may be further clarified in new legislation currently under consideration. More than one person can have parental responsibility for a child at the same time. It cannot be transferred or surrendered, but aspects of parental responsibility can be delegated (CA 1989 s. 2 (9)). See Chapter 11 for further details. (For the equivalent provisions in Scotland, see Sections 1–3 of the Children (Scotland) Act 1995.)

Patient-identifiable information   Facts or professional opinions about a client or patient learned in a professional capacity and from which the identity of the individuals concerned can be identified.

Personal data   Information relating to a specific individual.

Processing   Defined in section 1 (1) of the Data Protection Act 1998 to mean, in relation to information or data, obtaining, recording or holding the information or data or carrying out any operation or set of operations on the information or data, including: (a) organisation, adaptation or alteration of the information or data; (b) retrieval, consultation or use of the information or data; (c) disclosure of the information or data by transmission, dissemination or otherwise making available, or (d) alignment, combination, blocking, erasure or destruction of the information or data.

Public interest   The interests of the community as a whole, or a group within the community or individuals.

Relevant filing system   Defined in section 1 (1) of the Data Protection Act 1998 as any set of information that is structured either by reference to individuals or to criteria relating to individuals in such a way that specific information relating to an individual is readily accessible. In a relevant filing system, data about specific individuals can be located by a straightforward search.

Sensitive personal data   Defined in section 2 of the Data Protection Act 1998 as information about a specific individual which relates to: racial or ethnic origin, political opinions, religious beliefs or other beliefs of a similar nature, trade union membership, physical or mental health condition, sexual life, criminality (alleged or proven), and criminal proceedings, their disposal and sentencing.

Soft law   A term used to describe guidance, departmental circulars, codes of practice, charters, memoranda of understanding and recommendations in departmental and inter-departmental reports.

Supervision In the psychoanalytic tradition and in most therapeutic approaches in the USA, supervision is seen as supporting trainees who, on completion of their training, may work unsupervised. In Britain there is a tradition of independent supervision which continues throughout the training and the working life of the therapist, in which the supervisor is regarded as an independent facilitator with a specific role to support and mentor professional practice.

References and Further Reading

BACP (2002) *Ethical Framework for Good Practice in Counselling and Psychotherapy*. Rugby: British Association for Counselling and Psychotherapy.

BACP (2007) *Ethical Framework for Good Practice in Counselling and Psychotherapy*. Lutterworth: British Association for Counselling and Psychotherapy.

BMA (2000) *Consent, rights and choices in health care for children and young people*. London: BMA.

BMA and the Law Society (2003) *Assessment of Mental Capacity: Guidance for Doctors and Lawyers*. Available from BMJ Bookshop, Tel: 020 7383 6286, www.bma.org.uk/ethics

Bond, T. (1990) Counselling supervision – ethical issues. *Counselling, Journal of the British Association for Counselling*, 1(2): 43–46.

Bond, T. (2000) *Standards and Ethics for Counselling in Action* (second edition). London: SAGE.

Bond, T. (2004) *Ethical Guidelines for Researching Counselling and Psychotherapy*. Rugby: British Association for Counselling and Psychotherapy.

Bond, T., & Sandhu, A. (2005) *Therapists in Court: Providing Evidence and Supporting Witnesses*. London: SAGE.

BPS (2005) *Professional Practice Guidelines for Counselling Psychologists*. Leicester: British Psychological Society.

BPS (2006) *Code of Ethics and Conduct*. Leicester: British Psychological Society.

Brazier, M. (2003) *Medicine, Patients and the Law*. London: Penguin.

Cohen, K. (1992) Some legal issues in counselling and psychotherapy. *British Journal of Guidance and Counselling*, 20 (1): 10–26.

Crown Prosecution Service (England and Wales) (2005) *The CPS: Provision of Therapy for Vulnerable or Intimidated Adult Witnesses Prior to a Criminal Trial – Practice Guidance*. London: Crown Prosecution Service. Also available at www.cps.gov.uk

CWDC (2007) *ECM Common Assessment Framework Practitioners' and Managers' Guides: Guidance for Those Implementing and Using CAF*. Available online along with forms, supporting tools and factsheets at www.ecm.gov.uk/caf

DCA (2003a) *Making Decisions: DCA Guide for Healthcare Professionals*. Available on http://www.dca.gov.uk/legal-policy/mental-capacity/mibooklets/guide3.pdf

DCA (2003b) *Making Decisions: DCA Guide for Social Care Professionals*. Available on http://www.dca.gov.uk/legal-policy/mental-capacity/mibooklets/guide2.pdf

DCA (2003c) *Making Decisions: DCA Guide for Legal Practitioners*. Available on http://www.dca.gov.uk/legal-policy/mental-capacity/mibooklets/guide1.pdf

DCA (2003d) *Making Decisions: Helping People Who have Difficulty Deciding for Themselves. A guide for family and friends*. Available on http://www.dca.gov.uk/legal-policy/mental-capacity/mibooklets/guide4.htm

DfES (2004a) *Every Child Matters: Change for Children Programme*. Ref: DfES/1081/2004 www.everychildmatters.gov.uk. Norwich: TSO.

DfES (2004b) *Working with Voluntary and Community Organisations to Deliver Change for Children and Young People*. Norwich: TSO.

DfES (2004c) *National Service Framework (NSF) for Children, Young People and Maternity Services*. Norwich: TSO.

DfES (2004d) *Five Year Strategy for Children and Learners*. Norwich: TSO.

DfES (2004e) *Every Child Matters: Change for Children in Schools*. Norwich: TSO.

DfES (2004f) *Every Child Matters: Change for Children in the Criminal Justice System*. Norwich: TSO.

DfES (2004g) *Every Child Matters: Change for Children in Health Services*. Norwich: TSO.

DfES (2006a) *What to Do if You are Worried that a Child is Being Abused*. Norwich: TSO.

DfES (2006b) *Information Sharing – A Practitioner's Guide*. Norwich: TSO.

DfES (2006c) *Working Together to Safeguard Children: A Guide to Inter-Agency Working to Safeguard and Promote the Welfare of Children*. Norwich: The Stationery Office. Available for download at http://www.everychildmatters.gov.uk/workingtogether/and from TSO.

DH (2000) *Framework for Assessment of Children in Need and their Families*. Norwich: TSO.

DH (2003a) *Confidentiality: NHS Code of Practice*. London: Department of Health.

DH (2003b) *Department of Health: Mental Health Act; Code of Practice* (second edition). Available from www.doh.gov.uk/pub/docs/doh/mhcop.pdf

DH (2006a) *Caldicott Guardian Manual, 2006* : DH Publications, PO Box 777, London, SE1 6XH, email: dh@prolog.uk.com. Available for download at http://www.dh.gov.uk/en/Publicationsandstatistics/Publications/Publications Policy AndGuidance/DH_062722 and htttp://www.connectingforhealth.nhs.uk/systemsandservices/infogov/policy/re sources/new guidance

DH (2006b) *Report on the Review of Patient-Identifiable Information*, Committee chaired by Dame Fiona Caldicott in 1997 (the Caldicott Committee). Report available from website http://www.doh.gov.uk/confiden/crep.htm . The Caldicott Principles are to be found at http://www.doh.gov.uk/confiden/cgmintro.htm.

Feldman, D. (2002) Civil Liberties and Human Rights in England and Wales. Oxford: Oxford University Press.

General Medical Council:

GMC (2000a) *Confidentiality: Frequently Asked Questions* http://www.gmcuk.org/guidance/current/library/confidentiality_faq.asp

GMC (2000b) *Seeking patients' consent: The ethical considerations* http://www.gmcuk.org/guidance/current//library/consent.asp

GMC (2000c) *Accountability in Multi-disciplinary and Multi-Agency Mental Health Teams* http://www.gmc-uk.org/guidance/current/library/accountability_in_multi_ teams.asp

GMC (2004), (2000) *Confidentiality: Protecting and Providing Information* http://www.gmc-uk.org/guidance/archive/confidentiality_sep_2000.pdf http://www.gmc-uk.org/guidance/current/library/confidentiality.asp

GMC (2006) *Good Medical Practice*. Available at www.gmc-uk.org/guidance/current/library/confidentiality.asp http://www.gmc-uk.org/guidance/good_medical_practice/index.asp

Hershman A., & McFarlane, D. (2007a) *Children Law and Practice*. Bristol: Family Law

Hershman A., & McFarlane, D. (2007b) *Children Law Handbook*. Bristol: Family Law

IACP (2005) *Code or Ethics and Practice* (Information Sheet 7). Wicklow: Irish Association for Counselling and Psychotherapy.

Information Commissionor's Office (2005) *The impact assessment tools and handbook*. Available online at http://www.ico.gov.uk/global/search.aspx?collection=ico&keywords=impact+ assessment (accessed July 2008)

Institute of Psychiatry and Rethink (2006) *Sharing Mental Health Information with Carers: Pointers to Good Practice for Service Providers* (Briefing Paper). London: Department of Health.

Jackson, E. (2006) *Medical Law, Texts and Materials*. Oxford: Oxford University Press.

Law Commission (1981) *Breach of Confidence* (Cmnd 8388). London: HMSO.

Lord Laming (2003) *The Victoria Climbié Inquiry: Report of an Inquiry by Lord Laming*. Norwich: TSO.

Mason, J. K., & Laurie, G. T. (2006) *Mason and McCall Smith's Law and Medical Ethics* (seventh edition). Oxford: Oxford University Press.

Menowe, M. & McCall Smith, A. (eds) (1993) *The Duty to Rescue: Jurisprudence of AID*. Aldershot: Dartmouth.

Mitchels, B. (2007) 'About Courts' and 'Child Care Law' in *ABC of Child Protection*. London: BMJ & Blackstone Press.

Mitchels, B., & James, H. (2001) *Child Care and Protection: Law and Practice* (third edition). London: Cavendish.

Pattenden, R. (2003) *The Law of Professional-Client Confidentiality: Regulating the Disclosure of Confidential Personal Information*. Oxford: Oxford University Press.

Pattinson, S. D. (2006) *Medical Law and Ethics*. London: Sweet & Maxwell.

Proctor, B. (1986) Supervision: a co-operative exercise in accountability. In M. Marken & M. Payne (eds) *Enabling and Ensuring: Supervision in Practice*. Leicester: National Youth Bureau.

Reder, P., Duncan, S., et al (1994) *Beyond Blame: Child Abuse Tragedies Revisited*. London and New York: Routledge.

Secretary of State for the Home Department and Secretary of State Northern Ireland (1998) *Legislation Against Terrorism: A Consultation Paper* Cmnd 4178. Norwich: TSO.

Scottish Executive (2002) *Getting our Priorities Right*. Edinburgh: Scottish Executive.

Scottish Executive (2003a) *Sharing Information about Children at Risk*. Edinburgh: Scottish Executive.

Scottish Executive (2003b) "It's Everyone's Job to Make Sure I'm Alright": Report of the Child Protection Audit and Review. Edinburgh: Scottish Executive, http://www.scotland.gov.uk/library5/education/iaar.pdf

Scottish Executive (2003c) *Framework for Standards and Children's Charter*. Edinburgh: Scottish Executive.

Scottish Executive (2004a) *Protecting Children and Young People: The Charter*. Edinburgh: Scottish Executive, http://www.scotland.gov.uk/library5/education/ccel.pdf

Scottish Executive (2004b) *Protecting Children and Young People: The Framework for Standards*. Edinburgh: Scottish Executive, http://www.scotland.gov.uk/about/ED/CnF/00017834/page1423929284.pdf

Scottish Executive (2006) *Getting it Right for Every Child*. Edinburgh: Scottish Executive.

The Scottish Executive (2008a) *Interviewing Child Witnesses in Scotland*. Available at www.scotland.gov.uk/Publications/2003/09/18265/27033–14k

The Scottish Executive (2008b) *Code of Practice to Facilitate the Provision of Therapeutic Support to Child Witnesses in Court Proceedings*. Edinburgh: Scottish Executive.

The Scottish Office (1998a) *Protecting Children – A Shared Responsibility*. Guidance on Inter-Agency Co-operation. http://www.scotland.gov.uk/Topics/People/Young-People/children-families/17834/14723

The Scottish Office (1998b) *Protecting Children – A Shared Responsibility. Guidance for Health Professionals in Scotland*. http://www.scotland.gov.uk/Topics/People/Young-People/children-families/17834/14723

Trumble, W.R. & Stevenson, A. (eds) (2002) *The Shorter Oxford English Dictionary on Historical Principles*. Oxford: Oxford University Press.

Note: The Scottish Office and The Scottish Executive publications are available at www. scotland.gov.uk.

British Government publications are available from The Stationery Office (TSO) www.tsoshop.co.uk. TSO, PO Box 29, Norwich, NR3 1GN, Tel: 0870 600 5522, E-mail: customer.services@tso.co.uk

Useful internet sites

Courts and legal information relevant to capacity and consent

Enduring Powers of Attorney, explanatory booklet available from http://www.guardianship. gov.uk/formsdocuments/publications.htm EPA forms, available from website http://www.guardianship.gov.uk/downloads/ Make_An_EPA.Web.pdf in English; and in Welsh from http://www.legislation. hmso.gov.uk/

Lasting Power of Attorney From 1 October 2007, EPAs will be replaced by a Lasting Power of Attorney made under the Mental Capacity Act 2005. For information, please see website http://www.guardianship.gov.uk, which will carry the new forms when the new Act comes fully into force.

EPA Team, Public Guardianship Office, Archway Tower, 2 Junction Rd, London N19 5SZ. Email: pgoepa@guardianship.gsi.gov.uk Direct Fax: 020 7664 7705 Document Exchange: DX 141150 Archway2 London

High Court of Justice Address for correspondence; The Court Manager, Room E08, Royal Courts of Justice, The Strand, London, WC2A 2LL. Telephone: 020 7947 7309 (Customer Service Manager) Fax: 020 7947 7339 (Customer Service Manager) *In case of difficulty out of hours, contact the Royal Courts of Justice on 020 7947 6260.*

Addresses and contact numbers for other courts are to be found at: http://www.hmcourts-service.gov.uk/HMCSCourtFinder/

Scottish Courts http://www.scotcourts.gov.uk/

Websites providing information on consent, capacity and ethics

Adoption UK. 46 The Green, South Bar Street, Banbury, OX16 9AB. Tel: 01295 752240, Fax: 01295 752241, Helpline: 0844 848 7900 (10am to 4pm) http://www.adoptionuk.org

British Association for Adoption and Fostering http://www.baaf.org.uk/BAAF, Saffron House, 6-10 Kirby Street, London, EC1N 8TS, Phone: 020 7421 2600 Fax: 020 7421 2601. Email: mail@baaf.org.uk

British Medical Association http://www.bma.org.uk
Ethics: http://www.bma.org.uk/ap.nsf/Content/Hubethicshandbook
Children http://www.bma.org.uk/ap.nsf/Content/Hubethicschildren
Confidentiality http://www.bma.org.uk/ap.nsf/ Content/Hubethicsconfidentiality
Consent and capacity http://www.bma.org.uk/ap.nsf/Content/Hubethicsconsentandcapacity
Health Records http://www.bma.org.uk/ap.nsf/Content/ Hubethicshealthrecords
Human Rights http://www.bma.org.uk/ap.nsf/Content/HubethicshumanrightsReproduction
Issues http://www.bma.org.uk/ap.nsf/ Content/Hubethicsreproduction issues

General Medical Council:
Good medical practice www.gmc-uk.org/guidance/current/library/confidentiality.asp
http://www.gmc-uk.org/guidance/good_medical_practice/index.asp
Confidentiality: Protecting and Providing Information http://www.gmc-uk.org/guidance/ current/library/confidentiality.asp

Confidentiality: Frequently Asked Questions http://www.gmc-uk.org/guidance/current/ library/confidentiality_faq.asp

Seeking patients' consent: The ethical considerations http://www.gmc-uk.org/guidance/ current/library/consent.asp

Accountability in Multi-disciplinary and Multi-Agency Mental Health Teams http://www. gmc-k.org/guidance/current/library/accountability_ in_multi_teams.asp

Government Guidance on consent, capacity and ethics

Caldicott Guardian Manual, 2006.

Hard copies of this publication can be obtained from: DH Publications Orderline, PO Box 777, London, SE1 6XH, email: dh@prolog.uk.com quoting title "277311/The Caldicott Guardian Manual 2006". Also available for download at http://www.dh.gov.uk/en/ Publicationsandstatistics/Publications/PublicationsPolicyAndGuidance/DH_062722 and available on the internet at http://www. connectingforhealth.nhs.uk/systemsand services/infogov/policy/resources/ new_guidance

Report on the Review of Patient-Identifiable Information by the Caldicott Committee, chaired by Dame Fiona Caldicott in 1997. Report and principles available from website http://www.dh.gov.uk/en/index.htm

Information sharing practitioners' guide; Information sharing case examples; Information sharing further guidance on legal issues; Information sharing endorsements: Cross-Government Guidance to improve practice by giving practitioners across children's services clearer guidance on when and how they can share information legally and professionally. Available online at www.ecm.gov.uk/informationsharing http://www.everychildmatters. gov.uk/deliveringservices/informationsharing/

Lead professional practitioners' and managers' guides: Guidance for those implementing and carrying out lead professional functions. Available online at www.ecm.gov.uk

Supporting integrated working training strategy: Details of the outline training strategy and the range of training modules, including training in information sharing, are available at www.ecm.gov.uk/iwtraining

From 1 October 2007, the Children's Workforce Development Council (CWDC) took over responsibility from the DfES for implementation of integrated working. The CWDC website supports these areas. Enquiries by email should be directed to: integrated working@cwdcouncil.org.uk

Common Assessment Framework practitioners' and managers' guides: Guidance for those implementing and using CAF. Available online at www.ecm.gov.uk/caf

Department of Constitutional Affairs www.dca.gov.uk/legal-policy/mental-capacity/ guidance.htm

National Assembly for Wales, Information on guidance in Wales: www.wales.gov.uk/

NHS *The Information Governance Toolkit* www.igt.connectingforhealth.nhs.uk or nww.igt.con-nectingforhealth.nhs.uk. The IGT provides guidance on how organisations should satisfy confidentiality, data protection, information security, FOI, records management and information quality requirements. Extensive knowledgebase of exemplar documents, guidance materials and useful links: helpdesk@cfh.nhs.uk. An e-mail help line for assistance with the Information Governance Toolkit – content, technical advice and administration issues.

The Patient Information Advisory Group (PIAG)

http://www.advisorybodies.doh.gov.uk/piag. Provides the minutes of PIAG meetings and guidance on the use of powers provided under section 60 of the Health & Social Care Act 2001 which allow confidentiality requirements to be set aside in limited circumstances for purposes such as research and public health work. PIAG also provides guidance on issues of major significance that are brought to its attention and its guidance is published here.

Scottish Courts http://www.scotcourts.gov.uk/

References to Legal Cases

A v B plc and C ('Flitcroft') [2002] EWCA Civ 337; 3 WLR 542, reversing [2001] 1WLR 2341 ·
A.G. v Guardian Newspapers Ltd (No 2) [1990] AC 109 [1988] 3 All ER 477
A Health Authority v X [2001] EWCA Civ 2014; [2002] 2 All ER 780 (CA); affirming [2001] Lloyds Rep Med 349
A v Hoare and Others [2008] UKHL 6
Allen v British Rail Engineering CA 2001 EWCA Civ 242, [2001] ICR 942,
Attorney General v Guardian Newspapers (No 2) [1988] 3All ER 545
Boyd v US [1885] 116 US 616, 630
Campbell v Mirror Group Newspapers Ltd [2004] UKHL 22, [2004] 2 AC 457
Commissioner of Police v Ombudsman [1998] 1 NZLR 385
Douglas v Hello! [2007] UKHL 21
Durant v Financial Services Authority [2003] EWCA Civ 1746, (CA)
Gillick v West Norfolk and Wisbech Area Health Authority and Another [1986] 1 AC 1212; [1985] 3 All ER 402 (HL) [1986] 1 FLR 224; [1985] 1 All ER 533 (CA); [1985] 3 WLR 830
JD v Ross [1998] NZFLR 951
Kapadia v. London Borough of Lambeth [2000] (CA) 1 IRLR 699; 57 BMLR 170; The Times, 4 July 2000.
Lewis vs Prosthetists and Orthotists [2001] EWCA Civ 837
London Borough of Southwark v Afolabi [2003] ICR 800 CA,
Mr X v Hospital Z [1998] 8 SCC 296, 307
MS v Sweden [1999] 28 EHRR 313
R v Secretary of State for the Home Department, ex p Daly [2001] UKHL 26; [2001] 2AC 532
R v. Department of Health ex parte Source Informatics Ltd [2000] 1 All ER 786 CA; [1999] 4 All ER 185 QB.
Re L (Medical Treatment: Gillick Competency, [1998] 2 FLR 810, [1998] Fam Law 591
Re W (A Minor: Medical Treatment) [1992] 4 All ER 627
R v. the Secretary of State for the Home Department ex parte Daly [2001] UKHL 26; [2001] 2 AC 532
St George's Healthcare NHS Trust v S [1999] Fam 26
Sporrong v Sweden [1982] 5 EHRR 35
Tarasoff v The Regents of the University of California [1976] 551 P 2d 334 and [1974] 529 P 2d 553–554
W v Edgell and others [1990] 1 All ER 835; Ch 359 (CA) affirming [1989] 1 All ER 801
X v Y [1988] 2 All ER 648
Z v. Finland [1998] 25 EHRR 371

Acts and Rules cited in the text
Access to Health Records Act 1990
Access to Medical Reports Act 1988
Adoption and Children Act 2002
Adoption and Children (Scotland) Act 2007
Adoption Support Agencies (England) and Adoption Agencies (Miscellaneous Amendments) Regulations 2005, S.I. 2005/2720
Adoption Agencies Regulations 2005, S.I. 2005/389
Adoption Information and Intermediary Services Regulations (pre-commencement) 2005, S.I. 2005/890

Adoption Support Services Regulations 2005, S.I. 2005/691
Adults with Incapacity (Scotland) Act 2000
Age of Legal Capacity (Scotland) Act 1991
Children and Adoption Act 2006
Children Act 1989
Children Act 2004
Children Act 2004 Information Data Base [England] Regulations 2007, S.I. 2007/2182
Children (Scotland) Act 1995
Protection of Children and Prevention of Sexual Offences (Scotland) Act 2005
Children and Adoption Act 2006
Commissioner for Children and Young People (Scotland) Act 2003
Court of Protection Rules 2007. SI 2007 No 1744
Data Protection Act 1998
Data Protection (Processing of Sensitive Personal Data) Order 2000
Data Protection (Subjects Access Modification) (Health) Order 2000
Disclosure of Adoption Information (post-commencement adoptions) 2005/ S.I. 2005/888
Drug Trafficking Offences Act 1986
Drug Trafficking Act 1994
Education Act 2002
Family Law Act 1996
Family Proceedings Rules 1991, S.I. 1991/1247
Family Proceedings Courts (Children Act) Rules 1991, S.I. 1991/1395
Family Law Reform Act 1969
Fatal Accidents and Sudden Deaths Inquiry (Scotland) Act 1976
Freedom of Information Act 2000
Health and Social Care Act 2001
Health and Social Care (Community and Health and Standards) Act 2003
Human Fertilisation and Embryology Act 1990
Human Rights Act 1998
Inspection of Premises, Children and Records (Independent Schools) Regulations 1991, S.I.1991/975
Latent Damage Act 1986
Limitation Act 1980
Limitation (Scotland) Act 1973
Limitation (Scotland) Act 1984
Mental Capacity Act 2005
Mental Capacity Act 2005 (Appropriate Body) (England) Regulations 2006. SI 2006 No. 2810
Mental Health Act 1983
Mental Health Act 2007
Mental Health (Care and Treatment) (Scotland) Act 2003
Parental Responsibility Agreement Regulations 1991, S.I. 1991/1478
Police and Criminal Evidence Act 1984
Proceeds of Crime Act 2002
Protection of Children (Scotland) Act 2003
Protection of Children and Prevention of Sexual Offences (Scotland) Act 2005
Terrorism Act 2000
Vulnerable Witnesses (Scotland) Act 2004
Youth Justice and Criminal Evidence Act 1999

Useful Organisations and Contacts

Action on Elder Abuse Astral House, 1268 London Road, London SW16 4ER. Freephone helpline: 0880 8808 8042. www.elderabuse.org.uk

Adoption UK, 46 The Green, South Bar Street, Banbury, OX16 9AB Tel: 01295 752240, Fax: 01295 752241, Helpline: 0844 848 7900 (10am to 4pm). http://www.adoptionuk

Age Concern Astral House, 1268 London Road, London SW16 4ER. Tel: 020 8765 7200. www.ageconcern.org.uk

Alert 27 Walpole Street, London SW3 4QS. Tel: 020 7730 2800. www.donoharm. org.uk

Alzheimer's Society Gordon House, 10 Green Coat Place, London SW1P 1PH. Helpline: 0845 300 0336. www.alzheimers.org.uk

BAAF, British Association for Adoption and Fostering Saffron House, 6-10 Kirby Street, London, EC1N 8TS.Tel: 020 7421 2600, Fax: 020 7421 2601. Email: mail@baaf.org.uk http://www.baaf.org.uk/

British Association for Counselling and Psychotherapy BACP House, 15 St John's Business Park, Lutterworth, Leicestershire, LE17 4HB. Tel: 01455 883300, Fax: 01455 550243, Email bacp@bacp.co.uk. www.bacp.co.uk

British Medical Association, Tavistock Square, London WC1 9JP. Tel: 020 7383 6286, www.bma.org.uk

British Psychological Society St Andrews House, 48 Princess Road East, Leicester LE1 7DR. Tel: +44 (0)116 254 9568, Fax: +44 (0)116 227 1314, Email: enquiry@bps.org.uk www.bps.org.uk

CARERS UK Ruth Pitter House, 20–25 Glasshouse Yard, London EC1A 4JT. Carers Line Tel: 0808 808 7777; 020 7490 8824, www.carersonline.org.uk

Childrens' Trust http://www.thechildrenstrust.org.uk/

Commission for Health Care Audit and Inspection www.healthcarecommission.org.uk and also see www.opsi.gov.uk/

Commission for Social Care Inspection (CSCI) www.csci.org.uk/

Connexions http://www.connexions-direct.com/

Contact the Elderly 15 Henrietta Street, Covent Garden, London WC2E 8QG. Freephone: 0800 716543 www.contact-the-elderly.org

Court of Protection see Public Guardianship Office below.

Crown Prosecution Service (England and Wales) has headquarters in London and York, and operates under a structure of 42 areas in England and Wales. London Office: 7th Floor, 50 Ludgate Hill, London, EC4M 7EX. Tel: 020 7796 8000, Fax: 020 7710 3447.

Dementia Care Trust Kingsley House, Greenbank Road, Bristol BS5 6HE. Tel 0870 443 5325, 0117 952 5325. www.dct.org.uk

Dignity in Dying (formerly the Voluntary Euthanasia Society) 181 Oxford Street, London W1D 2JT. Tel: 0870 777 7868, http://www.dignityindying.org.uk/
Email: exit@euthanasia.cc

Down's Syndrome Association 155 Mitcham Road, London SW17 9PG. Tel: 020 8682 4001. www.downs-syndrome.org.uk

Foundation for People with Learning Disabilities 7th Floor, 83 Victoria Street, London, SW1H 0HW. Tel: 020 7802 0300. www.learningdisabilities.org.uk

General Medical Council 178 Great Portland Street, London W1W 5JE. General Enquiries Desk: 020 7580 7642. www.gmc-uk.org

Headway (brain injury association) 4 King Edward Court, King Edward Street Nottingham NG1 1EW. Helpline: 0808 800 2244, 0115 924 0800, (Nottingham); 020 7841 0240, (London). www.headway.org.uk

Help the Aged St James' Walk, Clerkenwell Green, London EC1R 0BE. Free welfare rights advice line Tel: 0808 800 6565. www.helptheaged.org.uk

Help the Hospices Hospice House, 34-44 Britannia Street, London WC1X 9JG. Helpline:0879 903 3 903. www.hospiceinformation.info

H.M. Chief Inspector of Education, Children's Services and Skills www.opsi.gov.uk/si/si2007/uksi_20070603_en.pdf

HM Revenue and Customs http://www.hmrc.gov.uk/menus/contactus.shtml

Learning and Skills Council www.lsc.gov.uk

Linacre Centre for Healthcare Ethics 60 Grove End Road, London NW8 9NH. Tel: 020 7806 4088. www.linacre.org

Manic Depression Fellowship Castle Works, 21 St George's Road, London, SE1 6ES. Tel: 020 7793 2600. www.mdf.org.uk

MedicAlert Foundation 1 Bridge Wharf, 156 Caledonian Road, London, N1 9UU. Tel: 0800 581 420. www.medicalert.org.uk

MENCAP 123 Golden Lane, London EC1Y 0RT. Helpline: 0808 808 1111, Tel: 020 7454 0454. www.mencap.org.uk

Mind (National Association for Mental Health) 15-19 Broadway, Stratford, London E15 4BQ. Tel: 020 8519 2122, Mind Infoline: 08457 660 163. www.mind.org.uk

Motor Neurone Disease Association PO Box 246, Northampton NN1 2P2. Tel: 01604 250505, Helpline: 08457 626262. www.mndassociation.org.uk

National Assembly for Wales, Information on guidance in Wales: www.wales.gov.uk/

National Autistic Society 393 City Road, London, EC1V 1NG. Tel: 020 7833 2299 Helpline: 0870 600 85 85. www.nas.org.uk

Official Solicitor 81 Chancery Lane, London, WC2A 1DD. Tel: 020 7911 7127. http://www.officialsolicitor.gov.uk/

Patient's Association PO Box 935, Harrow, Middlesex, HA1 3YJ. Tel: 020 8423 9119. Helpline: 0845 608 4455

Patient Concern PO Box 23732, London SW5 9FY. Tel: 020 7373 0794, www.patientconcern. org.uk

Patient Information Advisory Group (PIAG)
http://www.advisorybodies.doh.gov.uk/piag. Provides the minutes of PIAG meetings and guidance on the use of powers provided under section 60 of the Health & Social Care Act 2001 which allow confidentiality requirements to be set aside in limited circumstances for purposes such as research and public health work. PIAG also provides guidance on issues of major significance that are brought to its attention.

The Prevention of Professional Abuse Network POPAN, 1 Wyvil Court, Wyvil Road, London SW8 2TG. Tel: 020 7622 6334, Support line: 0845 4 500 300. www.popan.org.uk

Public Guardianship Office Archway Tower, 2 Junction Road, London N19 5SZ. Customer service helpline: 0845 330 2900, Enquiry Line: 0845 330 2900. www.guardianship.gov.uk

RESCARE (The National Society for mentally disabled people in residential çare) Third Floor, 24-32 Stephenson Way, London NW1 2HD. Helpline: 0808 808 0700. www.respond. org.uk

Respond Third Floor, 24-32 Stephenson Way, London, NW1 2HD. Helpline: 0808 808 0700. www.respond.org.uk

Rethink (formerly National Schizophrenia Fellowship) 17 Oxford Street, Southampton, SO14 3DJ. General Enquiries: 0845 456 0455, Advice Line: 020 8974 6814. www.rethink.org

SANE 1st Floor, Cityside House, 40 Alder Street , London E1 1EE. Helpline: 0845 767 8000. www.sane.org.uk

Scottish Voluntary Euthanasia Society http://www.euthanasia.cc/vess.html

Scope (Major disability charity with a focus on cerebral palsy) 6 Market Road, London N7 9PW. Tel: 020 7619 7257, Cerebral Palsy Helpline: 0808 800 3333. www.scope.org.uk

Speakability 1 Royal Street, London SE1 7LL. Tel: 020 7261 9572, Helpline: 080 8808 9572. www.speakability.org.uk

Solicitors for the Elderly PO Box 9, Peterborough PE4 7NN. Tel: 01733 326769. www.solicitorsfortheelderly.com

Stroke Association Stroke House, 240 City Road, London, EC1V 2PR. Tel: 020 7566 0300, Helpline: 0845 30 33 100. www.stroke.org.uk

Values into Action Oxford House, Derbyshire Street, London E2 6HG. Tel: 020 7729 5436. www.viauk.org

VOICE UK Wyvern House, Railway Terrace, Derby DE1 2RU. Tel: 01332 345346, Fax: 01332 295670, Email: voice@voiceuk.org.uk http://www.voiceuk.org.uk/

Index

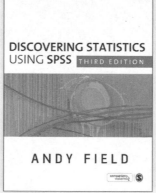
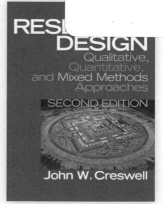